Algorithms

The Construction, Proof, and Analysis of Programs

Algorithms

The Construction, Proof, and Analysis of Programs

Pierre Berlioux
Institut National Polytechnique de Grenoble (ENSIMAG)

and

Philippe Bizard
Université Scientifique et Médicale de Grenoble

Translated by
Annwyl Williams

JOHN WILEY & SONS
Chichester · New York · Brisbane · Toronto · Singapore

First published 1983 © BORDAS, Paris under the title Algorithmique: construction, preuve et évaluation des programmes.

Library of Congress Cataloging in Publication Data:

Berlioux, Pierre.
Algorithms: the construction, proof, and analysis of programs.
Translation of: Algorithmique.
Bibliography: p.
Includes index.
1. Electronic digital computers—Programming.
2. Algorithms. I. Bizard, Philippe. II. Title.
QA76.6.B471913 1986 005.1 85–18000

ISBN 0 471 90844 4 (pbk.)

British Library Cataloguing in Publication Data:

Berlioux, Pierre
Algorithms: the construction, proof, and analysis of programs.
1. Electronic digital computers—Programming
2. Algorithms
I. Title II. Bizard, Philippe
001.64′2 QA76.6

ISBN 0 471 90844 4

Typeset by Photo·Graphics, Honiton, Devon
Printed and bound in Great Britain

Contents

Introduction

The sophist is content with appearances, the dialectician with proof; the philosopher seeks to know through examination and evidence.

JOSEPH JOUBERT

The substance of this book grew out of a teaching programme aimed at M.A. students in Computer Science at the Université Scientifique et Médicale de Grenoble and second-year engineering students at the Ecole Nationale Supérieure d'Informatique et de Mathématiques Appliquées de Grenoble.

It is addressed to those who already have some experience of programming and who, wishing to pursue the subject at a more advanced level, are interested in particular in the proof and analysis of programs.

We assume that the reader will be familiar with the fundamentals of programming, that he or she will have read, for example, textbooks by Arsac (1980), Biondi and Clavel (1981), Laurent (1982), Lucas, Peyrin and Scholl (1983), and Wirth (1977).

Our main aim, in this book, is to show how the construction, proof, and analysis of programs are all closely linked.

Chapter 1 introduces the basic elements which allow us to carry out the formal proof and analysis of iterative programs. We are thus able to prove that a given program satisfies the specification of the problem to be solved.

With the help of examples, Chapter 2 shows how one is led from these notions of proof towards the construction of correct programs, in particular through the definition of invariant properties.

Chapters 4 and 5, which deal with recursive programs, follow the same plan. In Chapter 5, we discuss the choice, for a given problem, of a recursive decomposition from which a correct recursive procedure can be constructed immediately.

Chapter 6 presents a method of transformation which allows us to convert a recursive program into an iterative program: the correctness of the more efficient version is assured by that of the original recursive program.

Chapter 3 gives a fuller account of the concepts introduced in Chapter 1, and is not essential to an understanding of the rest of the book. It can therefore be omitted at a first reading.

At the end of each chapter, there is a brief conclusion referring the reader either to basic articles and textbooks, or to other books which approach the subject from a different viewpoint. Of these, the most important are by Alagic and Arbib (1978), Arsac (1983), Dijkstra (1976), Gerbier (1977), Gries (1981), Mahl and Boussard (1983), Meyer and Baudoin (1978), and Wirth (1976).

The programs are written in a language close to Pascal. The elements necessary to an understanding of it are set out in Appendix 1.

For a presentation of the mathematical concepts, we refer the reader to Arbib *et al.* (1981), Greene and Knuth (1981), Kleene (1971), Liu (1977), and Stanat and McAllister (1977).

The courses corresponding to this book were given in Grenoble by Veillon (1974). We have also made use of the cyclostyled lecture notes of Courtin and Voiron (1974).

Notations

$\lceil x \rceil$ is the smallest integer y such that $y \geqslant x$.
$\lfloor x \rfloor$ is the largest integer y such that $y \leqslant x$.
$f(x)$ is of order $g(x)$ if and only if there are two strictly positive constants c_1 and c_2, such that for all x

$$c_1.g(x) \leqslant f(x) \leqslant c_2.g(x).$$

ln x is the natural logarithm of x.
C_n^p is the number of combinations of p objects taken n at a time.

The following notations are defined in the text, as indicated:

$E\{P\}S$	(section 1.2.1)	$wp(P, S)$	(section 3.1)
$\rightarrow$ & $\vee$ $\sim$ $\neg$	(section 1.2.2)	$sp(E, P)$	(section 3.1)
$C(x/y)$	(section 1.2.3.7)	π_x	(section 3.2.2)
W_C	(section 1.3.3)	$\bar{x}$	(section 3.4.1)
W	(section 1.4.1)	$\bar{\bar{x}}$	(section 6.3.1.2)
$W \times X$	(section 3.4.3)	H_n	(section 5.4.3.2)
f_P	(section 1.4.1)	$x \leqslant \alpha \leqslant y \rightarrow A(\alpha)$	(section 2.2.3.1)
$term_E P$	(section 3.1)		

Chapter 1

Proofs of Programs

1.1. Introduction

A program P defines an algorithm which maps a set of inputs L to a set of results R. In other words, for each $d \in L$, program P defines either a finite sequence of computations which gives a result $P(d) \in R$, or else an infinite sequence of computations, in which case the program is said to 'loop' for input d.

Program P has also been written in order to calculate a certain function f from $D \subseteq L$ to R. We say P is correct if and only if it computes f properly, that is if for each $d \in D$, $P(d)$ is defined (i.e. P does not loop for input d) and is equal to $f(d)$. The usual method for verifying that a program is correct involves testing: one chooses a finite sample of inputs $d_1, d_2, \ldots d_n$, and runs program P on each of them to verify that $P(d_1) = f(d_1)$, $P(d_2) = f(d_2), \ldots,$ $P(d_n) = f(d_n)$. The inadequacy of this method is obvious when the test sample does not exactly coincide with the set of inputs D (as is almost always the case, even when D is finite): for an input d which does not belong to the test sample, P can give an incorrect result even when it has given a correct result for each d_i of the sample. So one can never prove that a program is correct by testing. All one may perhaps prove is that it is incorrect, if for a value d_i of the sample $P(d_i) \neq f(d_i)$.

The method of program proving is a much more satisfactory one from a theoretical point of view: one shows that program P is correct by proving a theorem of the form: $\forall\ d \in D,\ P(d) = f(d)$.

We shall now proceed to examine a method of program proof, taking the following example as our illustration:

```
Div : r := a ; q := 0 ;
      while r ≥ b do
        begin
          r := r - b ;
          q := q + 1
        end
```

Here, a, b, q, and r are integer variables, where a and b have initial values which we shall denote by A and B. *Div* calculates, for $A \in \mathbb{N}$ and $B \in \mathbb{N}^+$, the quotient q and remainder r of the division of A by B. So for *Div* we have: $D = \mathbb{N} \times \mathbb{N}^+$, $R = \mathbb{N} \times \mathbb{N}$, and f is the function from $\mathbb{N} \times \mathbb{N}^+$ to $\mathbb{N} \times \mathbb{N}$ which associates with each pair (A, B) of $\mathbb{N} \times \mathbb{N}^+$ a pair (q, r) of $\mathbb{N} \times \mathbb{N}$ such that $A = Bq + r$ and $r < B$.

The proof that *Div* calculates this function correctly falls into two parts:

(a) *Proof of partial correctness*
We have to show that if *Div* terminates, then it gives a correct result.

(b) *Proof of termination*
We have to show that *Div* terminates for each input in $\mathbb{N} \times \mathbb{N}^+$.

1.2. Proofs of partial correctness

1.2.1

In the case of *Div*, we have to prove the following statement:

If, before the first instruction of *Div* is executed, variables a and b are initialized to values $A \in \mathbb{N}$ and $B \in \mathbb{N}^+$ respectively, then after *Div* is executed, the values of q and r will satisfy the conditions $A = Bq + r$, $r < B$, $r \geqslant 0$, $q \geqslant 0$.

We can express this statement formally as follows:

$$(a{=}A) \ \& \ (b{=}B) \ \& \ (A \geqslant 0) \ \& \ (B{>}0)$$
$$\{Div\}$$
$$(A{=}Bq{+}r) \ \& \ (q{\geqslant}0) \ \& \ (r{\geqslant}0) \ \& \ (r{<}B).$$

As a general rule, the statements which one will seek to prove during the course of a proof of partial correctness will take the form $E\{P\}S$, where E and S are predicates and P is a sequence of instructions (in particular, a complete program), the meaning being: if E is true before execution of P, and if P terminates, then S is true after execution. We shall call E the *precondition* and S the *postcondition* of P.

1.2.2. Predicates

Here we are dealing with expressions which can assume the values true or false. They will include relations between variables of the program (for instance, $a = bq+r$, $q \geqslant 0$, $b^2 - 4ac > 0$, etc. . . .) which may possibly be combined using the operations of Boolean algebra ($\neg$ (not), & (and), $\vee$ (or), $\rightarrow$ (implies), $\sim$ (equivalence)).

$a \rightarrow b$ is equivalent to $\neg a \vee b$, and also **if** a **then** b **else** *true*. Its truth table is therefore:

a \ b	*true*	*false*
true	*true*	*false*
false	*true*	*true*

$a \sim b$ denotes $(a \rightarrow b)$ & $(b \rightarrow a)$. Its truth table is therefore:

a \ b	*true*	*false*
true	*true*	*false*
false	*false*	*true*

In what follows, we shall write predicates with the following precedence rules for operations:

Highest precedence	$\neg$
↓	&
	$\vee$
Lowest precedence	$\rightarrow$, $\sim$

Remark
We note the following properties of the predicates *true* and *false*: for every program P and predicate C we have:

$$\textit{false}\ \{P\} C \quad \text{and} \quad C\{P\}\ \textit{true}$$

1.2.3. Axioms and deduction rules for proofs of partial correctness

A proof will always consist in deriving a *theorem* from a certain number of *axioms* by using *deduction rules*. In proofs of partial correctness, axioms and theorems will be statements of the form $E\{P\}S$. Below is a list of axioms and deduction rules which allow us to prove theorems of the form $E\{P\}S$. To prove relations between predicates (for instance, $E_1 \sim E_2$, $E_1 \rightarrow E_2$, etc. . . .) we shall use properties of Boolean algebra and properties of the domains of definition of the program variables (e.g. integers in the case of *Div*).

1.2.3.1. *Precondition rule*

if $E\{P\}S$
and $E' \rightarrow E$, then $E'\{P\}S$

1.2.3.2. *Postcondition rule*

if $E\{P\}S$
and $S \rightarrow S'$, then $E\{P\}S'$

1.2.3.3. *'And' rule*

if $E\{P\}S$
and $E\{P\}S'$, then $E\{P\}S \mathbin{\&} S'$

1.2.3.4. *'Or' rule*

if $E\{P\}S$
and $E'\{P\}S$, then $E \vee E'\{P\}S$

1.2.3.5. *Sequential composition rule (';' rule)*

if $E\{P\}F$
and $F\{Q\}S$, then $E\{P\ ;\ Q\}S$

1.2.3.6. *Exercises*

Using the preceding rules, prove the following properties:
(i) If $E\{P\}S$ and $E'\{P\}S'$ are theorems, then so are $E \mathbin{\&} E'\{P\}S \mathbin{\&} S'$ and $E \vee E'\{P\}S \vee S'$.
(ii) If $E\{P\}F$ and $G\{Q\}S$ are theorems, and if $F \rightarrow G$, then $E\{P\ ;\ Q\}S$ is also a theorem.

1.2.3.7. *Assignment axioms*

Given an assignment instruction $x := expr$ and a postcondition S, we have the axioms $E\{x := expr\}S$, where E is obtained from S by substituting expression *expr* for all occurrences of x in S.

E is the weakest condition that the variables must satisfy before execution of the assignment statement, in order for S to be true afterwards.

Examples
$(xy \geqslant 0)\ \{z := x*y\}\ (z \geqslant 0)$
$(q+1 \geqslant 0)\ \{q := q+1\}\ (q \geqslant 0)$
$(\ (x+y)^2 = y)\ \{x := x+y\}\ (x^2 = y)$

Exercises
(1) (a) Using the ';' rule, prove that:
$(y = 2)\ \{x := y+1\ ;\ z := x+y\}\ (z = 5)$
(b) Using the precondition rule, prove that:
$(q \geqslant 0)\ \{q := q+1\}\ (q \geqslant 0)$

(2) The substitution used in the above rule for assignment can also be denoted by $E = S(x/expr)$. In the special case of a conditional expression, this substitution is defined as follows:
$S(x/\textbf{if } a \textbf{ then } e_1 \textbf{ else } e_2) =_{df} (a \ \& \ S(x/e_1)) \vee (\neg a \ \& \ S(x/e_2))$
Use the preceding rule, generalized in this way, to show that:
$(z \geqslant 0) \ \{z := \textbf{if } b > 0 \textbf{ then } z+b \textbf{ else } z-b\} \ (z \geqslant 0)$

Important remark

Using the above assignment axiom, we can find a precondition of an assignment statement, given a postcondition, but not the other way round. Hence program proofs will be carried out in the following direction: we begin at the end (the postcondition) and work back towards the beginning (the precondition). In Chapter 3 will be found other rules for the formation of assignment axioms which will allow us to find a postcondition from a precondition and so to carry out program proofs in the other direction, starting at the beginning and working through to the end.

1.2.3.8. *Conditional rule*

1. if $E \ \& \ B\{P\}S$
   and $E \ \& \neg B \rightarrow S$, then $E\{\textbf{if } B \textbf{ then } P\}S$
2. if $E \ \& \ B\{P\}S$
   and $E \ \& \neg B\{Q\}S$, then $E\{\textbf{if } B \textbf{ then } P \textbf{ else } Q\}S$

Remark

In order to apply one of the above rules, it must be possible to consider test B purely as a predicate. It is therefore essential that the evaluation of B does not modify the values of the program variables.

1.2.3.9. *While-loop rule*

if $E \ \& \ B\{P\}E$, then $E\{\textbf{while } B \textbf{ do } P\}E \ \& \neg B$

As with the conditional rule, it must be possible to consider test B as a predicate without side-effects.

Condition E is called an *invariant* of the loop.

One of the difficulties of program proofs is finding an appropriate invariant for each loop (i.e. an invariant which will allow us to prove what it is that we wish to show). There is no systematic and general procedure for finding such invariants. One simply has to use intuition and understand the program in question.

1.2.3.10. *Rule for compound statements*

if $E\{P\}S$, then $E\{\textbf{begin } P \textbf{ end}\}S$

1.2.4. Proof of partial correctness of Div

We wish to prove (see §1.2.1):
$(a=A)$ & $(b=B)$ & $(A\geqslant 0)$ & $(B>0)$
$\{Div\}$
$(A=Bq+r)$ & $(q\geqslant 0)$ & $(r\geqslant 0)$ & $(r<B)$
Notice that:
$(a=A)$ & $(b=B)$ & $(A\geqslant 0)$ & $(B>0) \rightarrow (a=A)$ & $(b=B)$ & $(a\geqslant 0)$ & $(b>0)$
and
$(a=A)$ & $(b=B)$ & $(a=bq+r)$ & $(q\geqslant 0)$ & $(r\geqslant 0)$ & $(r<b) \rightarrow (A=Bq+r)$ & $(q\geqslant 0)$ & $(r\geqslant 0)$ & $(r<B)$

According to the rules of precondition and postcondition, it follows that all we have to prove is:
(I) $(a=A)$ & $(b=B)$ & $(a\geqslant 0)$ & $(b>0)$
$\{Div\}$
$(a=A)$ & $(b=B)$ & $(a=bq+r)$ & $(q\geqslant 0)$ & $(r\geqslant 0)$ & $(r<b)$

The proof is in two stages:
(a) $(a=A)$ & $(b=B)$ $\{Div\}$ $(a=A)$ & $(b=B)$
(b) $(a \geqslant 0)$ & $(b > 0)$ $\{Div\}$ $(a = bq+r)$ & $(q \geqslant 0)$ & $(r \geqslant 0)$ & $(r < b)$

(a) $(a=A)$ & $(b=B)$ $\{Div\}$ $(a=A)$ & $(b=B)$
Let us show first of all that $(a=A)$ & $(b=B)$ is an invariant of the loop.
We have (assignment rule):
$(a=A)$ & $(b=B)$ $\{q := q+1\}$ $(a=A)$ & $(b=B)$
$(a=A)$ & $(b=B)$ $\{r := r-b\}$ $(a=A)$ & $(b=B)$
Hence (composition rule):
$(a=A)$ & $(b=B)$ $\{r := r-b\ ;\ q := q + 1\}$ $(a=A)$ & $(b=B)$
Now $(a=A)$ & $(b=B)$ & $(r \geqslant b) \rightarrow (a=A)$ & $(b=B)$
Hence (precondition rule):
$(a=A)$ & $(b=B)$ & $(r\geqslant b)$ $\{r := r-b\ ;\ q := q + 1\}$ $(a=A)$ & $(b=B)$
from which we deduce (while loop rule):
(1) $(a=A)$ & $(b=B)$
{**while** $r \geqslant b$ **do begin** $r := r-b$; $q := q + 1$ **end**}
$(a=A)$ & $(b=B)$ & $(r < b)$
Applying the assignment and composition rules again, we find:
(2) $(a=A)$ & $(b=B)$ $\{r := a\ ;\ q := 0\}$ $(a=A)$ & $(b=B)$
From (1) and (2) we get (composition rule):
$(a=A)$ & $(b=B)$ $\{Div\}$ $(a=A)$ & $(b=B)$ & $(r < b)$
and finally, according to the postcondition rule:
$(a=A)$ & $(b=B)$ $\{Div\}$ $(a=A)$ & $(b=B)$

(b) $(a \geqslant 0)$ & $(b > 0)$ $\{Div\}$ $(a = bq+r)$ & $(q \geqslant 0)$ & $(r \geqslant 0)$ & $(\mathrm{r} < \mathrm{b})$

(b.1) First let us establish that $(a{=}bq{+}r)$ & $(q \geqslant 0)$ & $(r \geqslant 0)$ is an invariant of the loop. We have (assignment rule):

$(a{=}b(q{+}1){+}r)$ & $(q{+}1 \geqslant 0)$ & $(r \geqslant 0)$
$\{q := q{+}1\}$
$(a{=}bq{+}r)$ & $(q \geqslant 0)$ & $(r \geqslant 0)$

and $(a{=}b(q{+}1){+}r{-}b)$ & $(q{+}1 \geqslant 0)$ & $(r{-}b \geqslant 0)$
$\{r := \mathrm{r{-}b}\}$
$(a{=}b(q{+}1){+}r)$ & $(q{+}1 \geqslant 0)$ & $(r \geqslant 0)$

which gives (composition rule):

(3) $(a{=}b(q{+}1){+}r{-}b)$ & $(q{+}1 \geqslant 0)$ & $(r{-}b \geqslant 0)$
$\{r := r{-}b\ ;\ q := q{+}1\}$
$(a{=}bq{+}r)$ & $(q \geqslant 0)$ & $(r \geqslant 0)$

Looking at the precondition, we note:

(i) $(a{=}b(q{+}1){+}r{-}b)$ & $(q{+}1 \geqslant 0)$ & $(r{-}b \geqslant 0) \sim (a{=}bq{+}r)$ & $(q \geqslant -1)$ & $(r \geqslant b)$
(ii) Since $(q \geqslant 0) \rightarrow (q \geqslant -1)$
and $(r \geqslant 0)$ & $(r \geqslant b) \rightarrow (r \geqslant b)$
we have:

$(a{=}bq{+}r)$ & $(q \geqslant 0)$ & $(r \geqslant 0)$ & $(r \geqslant b) \rightarrow (a{=}bq{+}r)$ & $(q \geqslant -1)$ & $(r \geqslant b)$

Statement (3) therefore becomes (precondition rule):

$(a{=}bq{+}r)$ & $(q \geqslant 0)$ & $(r \geqslant 0)$ & $(r \geqslant b)$
$\{r := r{-}b\ ;\ q := q{+}1\}$
$(a{=}bq{+}r)$ & $(q \geqslant 0)$ & $(r \geqslant 0)$

and it follows that (loop rule):

(4) $(a{=}bq{+}r)$ & $(q \geqslant 0)$ & $(r \geqslant 0)$
{**while** $r \geqslant b$ **do begin** $r := r{-}b\ ;\ q := q{+}1$ **end**}
$(a{=}bq{+}r)$ & $(q \geqslant 0)$ & $(r \geqslant 0)$ & $(r < b)$

(b.2) Now let us use the specified loop invariant as a postcondition for the first instructions of the sequence.

We have (assignment rule):

$(a{=}b.0{+}r)$ & $(0 \geqslant 0)$ & $(r \geqslant 0)$
$\{q := 0\}$
$(a{=}bq{+}r)$ & $(q \geqslant 0)$ & $(r \geqslant 0)$

and $(a{=}b.0{+}r)$ & $(0 \geqslant 0)$ & $(r \geqslant 0) \sim (a{=}r)$ & $(r \geqslant 0)$

Applying the assignment rule once more, we get:

$(a{=}a)$ & $(a \geqslant 0)$ $\{r := a\}$ $(a{=}r)$ & $(r \geqslant 0)$

and $(a{=}a)$ & $(a \geqslant 0) \sim (a \geqslant 0)$

According to the composition rule, we have:

(5) $(a \geqslant 0)$ $\{r{:=}a\ ;\ q{:=}0\}$ $(a = bq{+}r)$ & $(q \geqslant 0)$ & $(r \geqslant 0)$

The composition rule, applied to (4) and (5), gives:

$(a \geqslant 0)$ $\{Div\}$ $(a{=}bq{+}r)$ & $(q \geqslant 0)$ & $(r \geqslant 0)$ & $(r < b)$

and the precondition rule allows us to conclude:

$(a \geqslant 0)$ & $(b > 0)$ $\{Div\}$ $(a = bq+r)$ & $(q \geqslant 0)$ & $(r \geqslant 0)$ & $(r < b)$
Having established (a) and (b), we can immediately deduce (I) from the 'and' rule (see exercise 1.2.3.6). *This proves the partial correctness of Div.*

1.3. Proofs of termination

1.3.1. Proof of termination of a program

A non-recursive program with no **goto** instructions will only produce an infinite sequence of computations if it executes the body of some loop an infinite number of times. Proving such a program terminates for each input $d \in D$ amounts therefore to showing that *each loop of the program can only be executed a finite number of times, for all* $d \in D$.

Take a loop '**while** B **do** P' (where the execution of P has already been shown to have terminated). Let $x_1, x_2, \ldots, x_n$ be the program variables. Let W_C denote the set of values of the vector $w = \langle x_1, x_2, \ldots, x_n \rangle$ satisfying a given condition C.

Let E be an invariant assertion of the loop, one that has been satisfied prior to execution.

Let w_1 belonging to W_E be the value of w before execution. If w_1 belongs to $W_{E\&\neg B}$, the loop terminates. Otherwise, w_1 belongs to $W_{E\&B}$, and after the body of loop P is executed, w has a value w_2 which belongs to W_E. If w_2 belongs to $W_{E\&\neg B}$, the loop terminates. Otherwise, after the execution of P, w has a value w_3 which belongs to W_E. Etc. . . .

To prove the termination of the loop, all we therefore have to do is to show that each sequence $w_1, w_2, w_3, \ldots$ constructed in this way is finite.

One method of doing this consists in defining a function m, from $W_{E\&B}$ to $\mathbb{N}$, for which one can show that

$$E \;\&\; B \;\&\; (m(w) = m_0)\ \{P\}\ \neg B \vee (m(w) < m_0) \qquad \forall m_0 \in \mathbb{N}$$

This states that if w has a value w_i before the execution of P, then after the execution of P, either the loop terminates, or else w has a value w_{i+1} such that $m(w_{i+1}) < m(w_i)$.

For each sequence $w_1, w_2, \ldots,$ the sequence $m(w_1), m(w_2), \ldots$ is then strictly decreasing in $\mathbb{N}$, hence finite. This implies that the sequence $w_1, w_2, \ldots$ is finite, and so the loop terminates for each value of w which satisfies E (the termination of P having been proved beforehand).

1.3.2. Proof of termination of Div

The sequence *Div* involves a single loop:

while $r \geqslant b$ **do**
begin $r := r-b$; $q := q+1$ **end**

Clearly, the body of this loop always terminates.

The predicate $(b=B)$ is an invariant of the loop, and is satisfied prior to execution (see the proof of partial correctness, (a)). The same applies to the predicate $(r \geqslant 0)$ (and also to (b)).

Consider the set $W_1 = W_{(b=B)\ \&\ (r\geqslant 0)\ \&\ (r\geqslant b)}$ and let the function m: $W_1 \rightarrow \mathbb{N}$ be given by $m(w)=r$.

Remark
This choice of function reduces proof of termination to a demonstration that successive values of variable r are strictly decreasing.

As the last section suggests, we still have to prove that

(1) $(b=B)\ \&\ (r \geqslant 0)\ \&\ (r \geqslant b)\ \&\ (r=m_0)$
$\{r := r-b\ ;\ q := q+1\}$
$(r < b) \vee (r < m_0) \qquad \forall m_0 \in \mathbb{N}$

The assignment rule gives:

$$(r-b < m_0)\ \{r := r-b\ ;\ q := q+1\}\ (r < m_0) \qquad \forall m_0 \in \mathbb{N}$$

which leads, when the precondition and postcondition rules are applied, to:

(2) $(b=B)\ \&\ (r \geqslant 0)\ \&\ (r \geqslant b)\ \&\ (r=m_0)\ \&\ (r-b < m_0)$
$\{r := r-b\ ;\ q := q+1\}$
$(r < b) \vee (r < m_0) \qquad \forall m_0 \in \mathbb{N}$

Now

$$(b=B)\ \&\ (r=m_0)\ \&\ (r-b < m_0) \sim (b=B)\ \&\ (r=m_0)\ \&\ (m_0-B < m_0)$$
$$\sim (b=B)\ \&\ (r=m_0)\ \&\ (B > 0)$$

The predicate $B > 0$ is always true since $(A,B) \in D = \mathbb{N} \times \mathbb{N}^+$, and therefore:

$$(b=B)\ \&\ (r=m_0)\ \&\ (r-b < m_0) \sim (b=B)\ \&\ (r=m_0).$$

This allows (1) to be deduced directly from (2), so completing the proof of termination of *Div*.

Remark
This proof of termination of *Div*, $\forall d \in D$, cannot be generalized to: $\forall d \in L$. For instance, if $L = Z \times Z$, then *Div* loops if $B = 0$.

1.3.3. Exercise

Prove the termination of Div by using the function $m'(w) = \lfloor A/B \rfloor - q$, where $\lfloor A/B \rfloor$ is the integer part of the quotient A/B. Show that on exit from the loop, we have $m'(w) = 0$.

1.4. Analysis of iterative programs

1.4.1

The analysis of a program P consists in determining the time and the space required for its execution, that is:

A function $T_P : L \rightarrow \mathbb{R} \cup \{+\infty\}$ such that $\forall d \in L$, $T_P(d)$ is the execution time of program P for the input $d(T_P(d) = +\infty$ if the program loops).

A function $N_P : L \rightarrow \mathbb{N} \cup \{+\infty\}$ such that $\forall d \in L$, $N_P(d)$ is the number of store locations needed to execute program P with input d ($N_P(d)$ can be infinite if the program loops).

In this section, we will only be concerned with determining the execution time of programs constructed from basic instructions (namely, assignments) with the aid of ';', conditionals and 'while' loops.

Let f_P denote the partial function from L to the set of results R, as computed by program P, and W the set W_{true} of possible values of variables of P.

f_P can be extended to a mapping from W to W. Similarly, if P' is a sequence of instructions from P, then the function $f_{P'}$ can also be defined as a mapping from W to W.

Example
In the case of *Div*, if $L = D$, $W = \mathbb{N} \times \mathbb{N}^+ \times \mathbb{N} \times \mathbb{N}$ = the set of possible values of a, b, q, and r, then $f_{Div}(a, b, q, r) = (a, b,$ quotient of a by b, remainder of a by $b)$. If we consider the instruction $q := q+1$ of *Div*, then

$$f_{q:=q+1}(a, b, q, r) = (a, b, q+1, r)$$

The execution time of a program can now be defined as follows:

(1) Each basic instruction and each condition has an execution time independent of the value of the variables. Hence, $\forall w \in W$,
   For each assignment $x := y$, $T_{x:=y}(w) =$ constant.
   For each condition B, $T_B(w) =$ constant.
   (Subsequently these constants will be written simply as $T_{x:=y}$ and T_B.)
(2) $T_{P;Q}(w) = T_P(w) + T_Q(f_P(w))$
(3) $T_{\textbf{if B then } P}(w) = \text{if } B \text{ then } (T_B + T_p(w)) \text{ else } T_B$

   $T_{\textbf{if B then } P \textbf{ else } Q}(w) = \text{if } B \text{ then } (T_B + T_p(w)) \text{ else } (T_B + T_Q(w))$

(4) $T_{\textbf{while B do } P}(w) = (n(w)+1)T_B + \sum_{i=0}^{n(w)-1} T_p(f_P^i(w))$

   where n is a function from W to $\mathbb{N} \cup \{+\infty\}$ such that $n(w)$ is the number of times P is executed for initial value w.

1.4.2. Execution time of *Div*

The number of traversals of the loop is the final value of variable q, that is $\lfloor A/B \rfloor$, the integer part of the quotient of A by B, where A and B are the inputs of *Div* (see exercise 1.3.3). Moreover, the execution time for the body of the loop is independent of the inputs and equal to $T_{r:=r-b} + T_{q:=q+1}$.

So we have:

$$T_{Div}(A,B) = T_{r:=a} + T_{q:=0} + (\lfloor A/B \rfloor + 1)\, T_{r\geqslant b} + \lfloor A/B \rfloor\, (T_{r:=r-b} + T_{q:=q+1})$$

$T_{Div}(A,B)$ is therefore of the form $K_1\lfloor A/B\rfloor + K_2$, where K_1 and K_2 are independent of the inputs A and B. $T_{Div}(A,B)$ is hence of order $\lfloor A/B\rfloor$.

Remark
One is often interested in the order of magnitude of T_P rather than the function itself, which depends on the hardware and the logical apparatus used to execute program P. It is sufficient, therefore, to determine the number of times the most frequently executed sequence of instructions of the program is executed. This number is obtained by counting the number of traversals of each loop.

Comments and Bibliography

The method we have presented for the proof of partial correctness of programs is due to Hoare (1969), and is based on the method of Floyd (1967). It describes a system of formal logic, Hoare logic, a more precise definition of which can be found in the article by Apt (1981). For the basic concepts of mathematical logic, consult, for example, the book by Kleene (1971). Proofs in a formal system are too long and detailed to be feasible in practice, at least without the help of an automatic theorem-proving program.

We shall see in Chapter 2 how to make practical use of program proofs in the construction of correct programs.

Chapter 2

Application to the Construction of Programs

2.1. Introduction

The last chapter showed how difficult and tiresome it is to prove a program, even a very short and simple one. In fact, the amount of work which has to be done to prove an existing program correct severely limits the scope of such a method. But it does suggest a more efficient procedure, one which allows a program and its proof to be conceived at the same time. For example, a loop can be specified by an invariant before it is constructed, the termination condition can be determined from its postcondition, and the body of the loop can be written in such a way that it maintains the invariant and is only executed a finite number of times. As a first example of this programming method, we shall outline a program for calculating the greatest common divisor of two positive integers, using the following arithmetic properties:

$$\begin{array}{ll} \text{if } a = b & \mathrm{GCD}(a,b) = a = b \\ \text{if } a < b & \mathrm{GCD}(a,b) = \mathrm{GCD}(a,b-a) \\ \text{if } a > b & \mathrm{GCD}(a,b) = \mathrm{GCD}(a-b,b). \end{array}$$

Let A and B be the inputs of the program, and let a and b be two program variables initialized to A and B. After this initialization, the condition $\mathrm{GCD}(a,b) = \mathrm{GCD}(A,B)$ is satisfied. If the rest of the program is a loop with invariant $\mathrm{GCD}(a,b) = \mathrm{GCD}(A,B)$ and termination condition $a = b$, then after executing such a loop we will have $\mathrm{GCD}(a,b) = a = b = \mathrm{GCD}(A,B)$; what we are trying to find out is therefore the final value of either of the two variables of a and b.

The body of the loop must be defined in such a way that, on the one hand the invariant is maintained, and on the other the loop is only executed a finite number of times. It is clear from the properties of GCD that if $a \neq b$, then the instruction **if** $a > b$ **then** $a := a - b$ **else** $b := b - a$ leaves the assertion $\mathrm{GCD}(a,b) = \mathrm{GCD}(A,B)$ invariant. It remains to be shown that this loop can only be executed a finite number of times. The loop condition being $a \neq b$, the instruction $b := b - a$ is executed only if $b > a$. The relation (a integer $>$ 0) & (b integer $>$ 0) is therefore also an invariant of the loop, and $max(a,b)$ is a strictly positive integer. Since $max(a,b)$ is strictly decreasing each time the body of the loop is executed, the loop always terminates.

We have therefore written the following program and informally proved it correct:

```
P :   while a ≠ b do
          if a > b then a := a − b else b := b − a;
      result := a
```

Exercises

(1) Carry out a formal proof for program P.
(2) Determine the maximum number of executions of the loop of P.
(3) Use the Div program in the last chapter to deduce from P a program to calculate the GCD of two positive integers A and B by calculating successive remainders.

2.2. The problem of the three-coloured flag

We are given:

(1) An array of N elements with indices from 1 to N, where each element is either a red, white or blue token.
(2) Predicates $B(i)$, $W(i)$ and $R(i)$ which are true if and only if the ith token ($1 \leqslant i \leqslant N$) is blue, white or red respectively.
(3) The primitive operation $swap(i,j)$ whose effect is to place the ith token at position j and the jth token at position i; $swap(i,j)$ is defined for all integers i and j between 1 and N. (Note: The case $i=j$ is not excluded).

The tokens have to be arranged in the order 'blue, white, red', and each of the predicates B, W, and R can be calculated at most once for each token. Moreover, on the assumption that the swap operation is expensive, we must try to use it as little as possible.

2.2.1. First solution

We use a while loop, whose invariant is represented by the following diagram, and whose loop condition is 'area X is empty'.

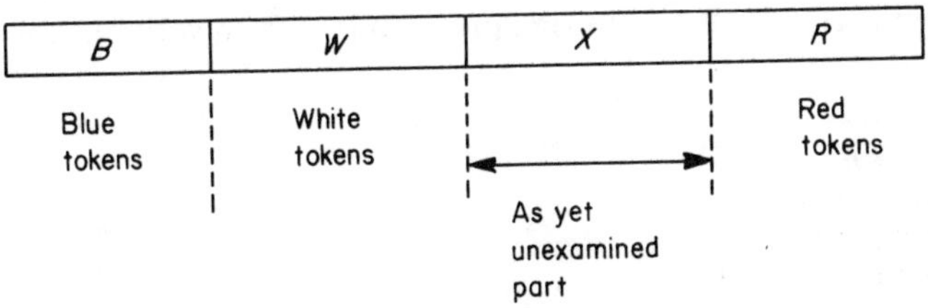

B	W	X	R
Blue tokens	White tokens	⟵ As yet unexamined part ⟶	Red tokens

Three indices, b, w, and r, are needed to separate the four areas of the array. We make the following choice: indices b and w point to the tokens which come immediately after areas B and W respectively. Index r points to the token which comes immediately before area R. (Discuss this choice.)

This gives the invariant:

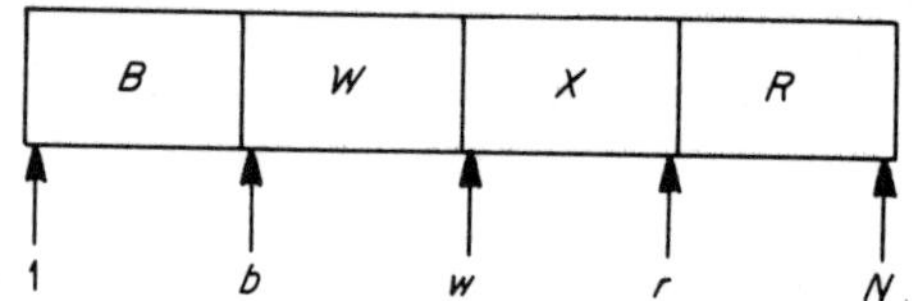

or equivalently:

$$P_{b,w,r} = (1 \leqslant \alpha < b \rightarrow B(\alpha))\ \&\ (b \leqslant \alpha < w \rightarrow W(\alpha))$$
$$\&\ (r < \alpha \leqslant N \rightarrow R(\alpha))$$

The postcondition of the program is then:

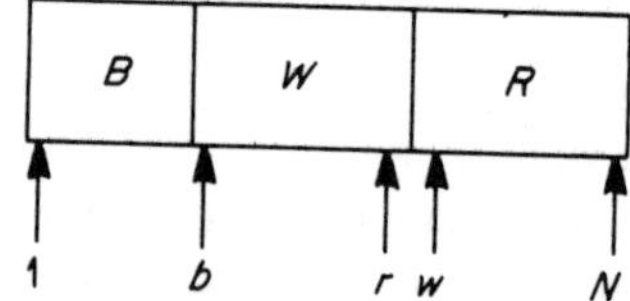

or equivalently:

$$P_{b,w,r}\ \&\ (w = r+1)$$

The program will therefore take the following form:

{Initialization : $P_{b,w,r}$ true}
while area X not empty **do**
  {body of loop with invariant $P_{b,w,r}$}

We have to verify after executing such a program that

$$P_{b,w,r}\ \&\ (\text{area } X \text{ is empty})$$

from which it follows that the array is sorted in the required manner. Consider in particular the following program (in which variable n is initialized to N):

(I)

```
w := b := 1 ; r := n ;
while w ≤ r do
if W(w) then w := w + 1
else if B(w) then
     begin swap(b,w) ; b := b + 1 ; w := w + 1 end
     else
     begin swap(r,w) ; r := r − 1 end
```

Verify that this program satisfies the constraint concerning the calculation of predicates B, W, and R.

A proof of this program can be found in section 2.2.3.

Analysis

Number of times the loop is executed = N

Number of swaps = $ne_1 = \#B + \#R$

($\#B$ = number of blue tokens)
($\#R$ = number of red tokens)

These results are not optimal. For example, we can try to decrease the number of exchanges involving the red tokens, as in the following program:

(Ib)

```
w := b := 1 ; r := n ;
while w ⩽ r do
if W(w) then w := w + 1
else    if B(w) then
        begin swap(b,w) ; b := b + 1 ; w := w + 1 end
        else
        begin while R(r) and w < r do r := r − 1 ;
              swap (r,w) ; r := r − 1
        end
```

2.2.2. Second solution

We use the invariant represented by:

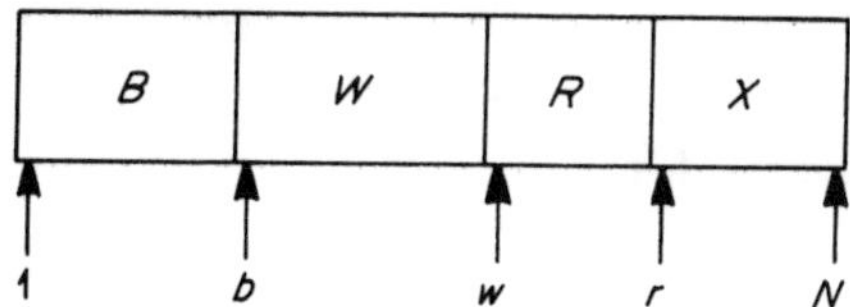

from which the following program can be derived (this will be verified informally, since the proof is fairly long):

(II)

```
b := w := r := 1 ;
while r ⩽ n do
if R(r) then r := r+1
else    if W(r) then
        begin swap(w,r) ; w := w+1 ; r := r+1 end
        else
        begin swap(w,r) ; r := r+1 ;
              swap(b,w) ; b := b+1 ; w := w+1
end
```

Analysis
Number of times the loop is executed = N
Number of swaps = $ne_2 = \#W + 2\,\#B$

Comparing these results with those of program (I), we have:

$$ne_2 - ne_1 = \#B + \#W - \#R$$

Program (I) is hence preferable to program (II), unless at least half the tokens are red.

Exercise
(a) Explain, as in the last section, the meaning of b, w, and r, and the invariant chosen for program (II).
(b) Take the program:

(IIb)

```
b := w := r := 1 ;
while r ≤ n do
if R(r) then r := r+1
else     if W(r) then
         begin swap(w,r) ; w := w+1 ; r := r+1 end
         else
         begin swap(b,r) ; b := b+1 ;
               swap(w,r) ; w := w+1 ; r := r+1
         end
```

This program is incorrect.
Find an initial distribution of an array with two tokens which will reveal the error.
Verify that in this program the invariant specified in (a) is not maintained.

2.2.3. Proof of program (I) (see §2.2.1)

2.2.3.1. *Definitions and notations*

We constructed program (I) using an invariant which can be represented by:

$$P_{b,w,r} = (1 \leqslant \alpha < b \rightarrow B(\alpha)) \;\&\; (b \leqslant \alpha < w \rightarrow W(\alpha)) \\ \&\; (r < \alpha \leqslant N \rightarrow R(\alpha))$$

To prove the program, we shall simplify the notation, as follows:

$x \leqslant \alpha \leqslant y \rightarrow A(\alpha)$ is the shortened notation for:

$$\begin{cases} A(x) \;\&\; A(x+1) \;\&\; \ldots \;\&\; A(y) & \text{if } x \leqslant y \\ \textit{true} & \text{otherwise} \end{cases}$$

or equivalently:

$$(x \leqslant y) \rightarrow A(x) \ \& \ \ldots \ \& \ A(y)$$

Now let us specify the problem (described at the beginning of section 2.2) in terms of predicates:

(a) Conditions (1) and (2) can be expressed by:
$E_1 = (1 \leqslant \alpha \leqslant N) \rightarrow (B(\alpha) \vee W(\alpha) \vee R(\alpha))$

(b) Definition (3) of the primitive *swap(i,j)* leads to the following axiom:

'Given a postcondition S, we have:
$E \ \& \ (1 \leqslant i \leqslant N) \ \& \ (1 \leqslant j \leqslant N) \ \{swap(i,j)\} \ S$
where E is obtained from S by replacing:
each occurrence of $B(expr)$, $W(expr)$, $R(expr)$, where *expr* has value i, by $B(j)$, $W(j)$ and $R(j)$;
and each occurrence of $B(expr)$, $W(expr)$, $R(expr)$, where *expr* has value j, by $B(i)$, $W(i)$ and $R(i)$'.

(c) The postcondition of the program (the sorting of the array) can be expressed by:
$S_1 = (1 \leqslant b \leqslant N{+}1) \ \& \ (b{-}1 \leqslant r \leqslant N) \ \& \ (1 \leqslant \alpha < b \rightarrow B(\alpha))$
$\& \ (b \leqslant \alpha \leqslant r \rightarrow W(\alpha)) \ \& \ (r < \alpha \leqslant N \rightarrow R(\alpha))$.
The loop invariant that we have to use is therefore not simply $P_{b,w,r}$ but:
$Q_{b,w,r} = E_1 \ \& \ (1 \leqslant b \leqslant w) \ \& \ (w{-}1 \leqslant r \leqslant N) \ \& \ P_{b,w,r}$
Let A_1 denote the while loop of program (I) and A_2 its body.

2.2.3.2. *Proof of partial correctness*

Lemma $x \leqslant \alpha \leqslant y \rightarrow A(\alpha)$ is equivalent to:
$(x \leqslant \alpha \leqslant y{-}1 \rightarrow A(\alpha)) \ \& \ (x \leqslant y \rightarrow A(y))$

Proof
$(x \leqslant \alpha \leqslant y \rightarrow A(\alpha))$
$\sim (x \leqslant y) \rightarrow A(x) \ \& \ \ldots \ \& \ A(y)$ by definition
$\sim ((x < y) \rightarrow A(x) \ \& \ \ldots \ \& \ A(y)) \ \& \ ((x{=}y) \rightarrow A(y))$
$\sim ((x < y) \rightarrow A(x) \ \& \ \ldots \ \& \ A(y{-}1)) \ \& \ ((x < y) \rightarrow A(y))$
$\& \ ((x{=}y) \rightarrow A(y))$
$\sim (x \leqslant \alpha \leqslant y{-}1 \rightarrow A(\alpha)) \ \& \ ((x \leqslant y) \rightarrow A(y))$

(a) *Proof of the invariance of* $Q_{b,w,r}$ *in* A_2:
It can easily be verified that

$$E_1 \ \& \ (1 \leqslant i \leqslant N) \ \& \ (1 \leqslant j \leqslant N) \ \{swap(i,j)\} \ E_1$$

(i) In the case $W(w)$, we obviously have:

$$Q_{b,w+1,r} \ \{w := w{+}1\} \ Q_{b,w,r}$$

Now, $Q_{b,w,r}$ & $(w \leqslant r)$ & $W(w)$

$\sim E_1$ & $(1 \leqslant b \leqslant w)$ & $(w \leqslant r \leqslant N)$ & $P_{b,w,r}$ & $W(w))$

and $P_{b,w,r}$ & $W(w) \rightarrow P_{b,w+1,r}$.

Hence $Q_{b,w,r}$ & $(w \leqslant r)$ & $W(w) \rightarrow Q_{b,w+1,r}$. So we have shown:

$Q_{b,w,r}$ & $(w \leqslant r)$ & $W(w)$ $\{w := w+1\}$ $Q_{b,w,r}$

(ii) In the case $B(w)$, we obviously have:

$$Q_{b+1,w+1,r}\ \{b := b+1;\ w := w+1\}\ Q_{b,w,r}$$

Now

$$P_{b+1,w+1,r} = (1 \leqslant \alpha < b+1 \rightarrow B(\alpha))\ \&\ (b+1 \leqslant \alpha < w+1 \rightarrow W(\alpha))$$
$$\&\ (r \leqslant \alpha < N \rightarrow R(\alpha))$$

Hence, according to the lemma:

$$P_{b+1,w+1,r} \sim (1 \leqslant \alpha < b \rightarrow B(\alpha))\ \&\ (b+1 \leqslant \alpha < w \rightarrow W(\alpha))$$
$$\&\ (r < \alpha \leqslant N \rightarrow R(\alpha))$$
$$\&\ ((b \geqslant 1 \rightarrow B(b))\ \&\ ((w \geqslant b+1) \rightarrow W(w))$$

Let us apply to $Q_{b+1,w+1,r}$ the swap axiom:

$$F\{swap(b,w)\}\ Q_{b+1,w+1,r}$$

where:

$$F = E_1\ \&\ (1 \leqslant b+1 \leqslant w+1)\ \&\ (w \leqslant r \leqslant N)\ \&\ (1 \leqslant \alpha < b \rightarrow B(\alpha))$$
$$\&\ (b+1 \leqslant \alpha < w \rightarrow W(\alpha))\ \&\ (r < \alpha \leqslant N \rightarrow R(\alpha))$$
$$\&\ ((b \geqslant 1) \rightarrow B(w))\ \&\ (w \geqslant b+1)$$
$$\rightarrow W(b))\ \&\ (1 \leqslant b \leqslant N)\ \&\ (1 \leqslant w \leqslant N)$$

But $(b+1 \leqslant \alpha < w \rightarrow W(\alpha))$ & $((w \geqslant b+1) \rightarrow W(b)) \sim (b \leqslant \alpha < w \rightarrow W(\alpha))$, and so $F \sim E_1$ & $(1 \leqslant b \leqslant w)$ & $(w \leqslant r \leqslant N)$ & $B(w)$ & $P_{b,w,r}$.

From this we deduce: $Q_{b,w,r}$ & $(w \leqslant r)$ & $\neg W(w)$ & $B(w) \rightarrow F$ which proves:

$Q_{b,w,r}$ & $(w \leqslant r)$ & $\neg W(w)$ & $B(w)$ $\{swap(b,w);\ b{:=}b+1;\ w{:=}w+1\}$ $Q_{b,w,r}$

(iii) In the case $R(w)$, we have: $Q_{b,w,r-1}\ \{r{:=}r-1\} Q_{b,w,r}$. On the other hand, from the lemma we have:

$$P_{b,w,r-1} \sim P_{b,w,r}\ \&\ ((r \leqslant N) \rightarrow R(r))$$

Let us apply to $Q_{b,w,r-1}$ the swap axiom:

$$G\{swap\ r(r,w)\}\ Q_{b,w,r-1}$$

where $G = E_1$ & $(1 \leqslant b \leqslant w)$ & $(w-1 \leqslant r-1 \leqslant N)$ & $P_{b,w,r}$
& $((r \leqslant N) \rightarrow R(w))$ & $(1 \leqslant r \leqslant N)$ & $(1 \leqslant w \leqslant N)$
[in fact, we have

$P_{b,w,r}$ & $(b \leqslant w)$ & $(w \leqslant r)$ & $(1 \leqslant w \leqslant N)$ & $(1 \leqslant r \leqslant N)$
$\{swap(r,w)\}$
$P_{b,w,r}$ & $(b \leqslant w)$ & $(w \leqslant r)$]

We have $G \sim E_1$ & $(1 \leqslant b \leqslant w)$ & $(w \leqslant r \leqslant N)$ & $R(w)$ & $P_{b,w,r}$.
Now, E_1 & $\neg W(w)$ & $\neg B(w)$ & $(1 \leqslant w \leqslant N) \rightarrow R(w)$
and so, $Q_{b,w,r}$ & $(w \leqslant r)$ & $\neg W(w)$ & $\neg B(w) \rightarrow G$ which proves:

$Q_{b,w,r}$ & $(w \leqslant r)$ & $\neg W(w)$ & $\neg B(w)$
$\{swap(r,w)\ ;\ r{:=}r-1\}$ $Q_{b,w,r}$

From the above three results we can deduce:

$Q_{b,w,r}$ & $(w \leqslant r)$ $\{A_2\}$ $Q_{b,w,r}$

(b) *Proof of program(I)*
According to the preceding section:
$Q_{b,w,r}\{A_1\}$ $Q_{b,w,r}$ & $(w > r)$

(i) *Postcondition*
We have $Q_{b,w,r}$ & $(w > r) \rightarrow (1 \leqslant b \leqslant w)$ & $(w=r+1)$ & $(r \leqslant N)$ & $P_{b,w,r}$
and $P_{b,w,r}$ & $(w=r+1) \rightarrow (1 \leqslant \alpha < b \rightarrow B(\alpha))$ & $(b \leqslant \alpha \leqslant r \rightarrow W(\alpha))$
& $(r < \alpha \leqslant N \rightarrow R(\alpha))$
Hence $Q_{b,w,r}$ & $(w > r) \rightarrow S_1$, and so $Q_{b,w,r}$ $\{A_1\}$ S_1

(ii) *Initialization*
We have E_1 & $(0 \leqslant n \leqslant N)$ & $(n < \alpha \leqslant N \rightarrow R(\alpha))$
$\{w{:=}b{:=}1;\ r{:=}n\}$
$Q_{b,w,r}$
Now, $(n=N) \rightarrow (0 \leqslant n \leqslant N)$ & $(n < \alpha \leqslant N \rightarrow R(\alpha))$ and so E_1 & $(n=N)$
{program (I)} S_1
This completes the proof of partial correctness.

2.2.3.3. *Proof of termination* (see §1.3.1)

The only loop of program (I) is loop A_1 (the body of the loop being A_2). Let $X_1 = W_{Q_{bwr}\ \&\ (w \leqslant r)}$ and the function $m : X_1 \rightarrow \mathbb{N}$ be defined by $m(x) = r-w$.

Remark
The proof of termination consists in showing that the quantity $r-w$, and therefore the size of the unexamined area, decreases with each execution of A_2. To prove the termination of A_1, all we have to do is to show that:

$Q_{b,w,r}$ & $(w \leqslant r)$ & $(r-w=m_0)$ $\{A_2\}$ $(w > r) \vee (r-w < m_0)$

for all $m_0 \in \mathbb{N}$.

By observing that $(r-w=m_0)$ $\{w:=w+1\}$ $(r-w=m_0-1)$ if $W(w)$ and $B(w)$

and $(r-w=m_0)$ $\{r:=r-1\}$ $(r-w=m_0-1)$ if $R(w)$

it is easy to prove that:

$$Q_{b,w,r} \ \& \ (w \leqslant r) \ \& \ (r-w=m_0) \ \{A_2\} \ (r-w=m_0-1) \qquad \forall m_0 \in \mathbb{N}$$

Program (I) therefore terminates.

2.2.3.4. *Proof that program (I) satisfies the constraints imposed in the statement of the problem*

We have not so far proved that 'the predicates B, W, and R are each calculated at most once for each token'.

From the last section, we can deduce that A_2 is executed *exactly N times* (the value $r-w$ is decreased by 1 with each traversal from $N-1$ to 0). Now, one execution of A_2 calculates (once at most) the predicates associated with *one token only*. Since for sorting to be achieved, the colours of the N tokens must be known, and since there are N executions of A_2 altogether, each execution involves a different token.

The constraint on the predicates is therefore satisfied by program (I).

Exercises

(1) Prove that program (Ib) also satisfies the constraint.

(2) Prove that this is no longer true if the embedded loop in (Ib) is replaced by:

while $R(r)$ **and** $(w \leqslant r)$ **do** $r:=r-1$;
if $w < r$ **then begin** *swap*(r,w) ; $r:=r-1$ **end**

Show how this program can lead to the calculation of $R(0)$.

2.3. Printing a list in reverse order

We are given:

(a) A linear list whose elements have the following structure: **record** element (**string** contents; **pointer** (element) tail).

(b) A pointer *headoflist* which indicates the first element of the list.

We assume that the list contains at least one element (*headoflist* $\neq$ *nil*). The problem is to write a program which prints in reverse order the contents of the list. For example, if one has:

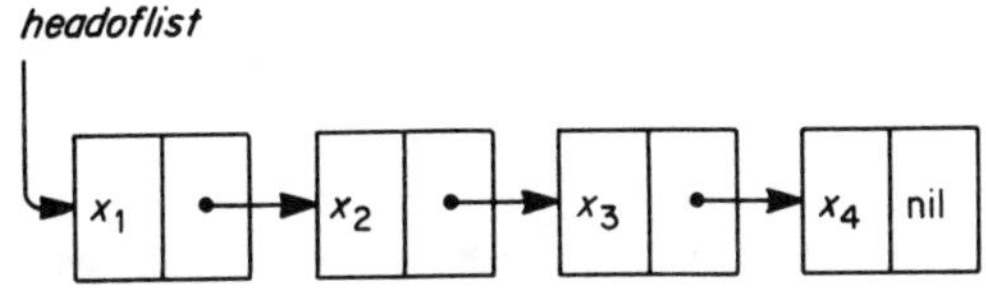

the program must print in succession x_4, x_3, x_2, x_1.

We shall give three solutions, PL1, PL2, and PL3. For each of these we shall analyse, as a function of n, the length of the list, the running time, and the storage space (over and above that required for the list itself) necessary for executing the program.

All three programs PL1, PL2, and PL3 will use a loop which admits an invariant of the form:

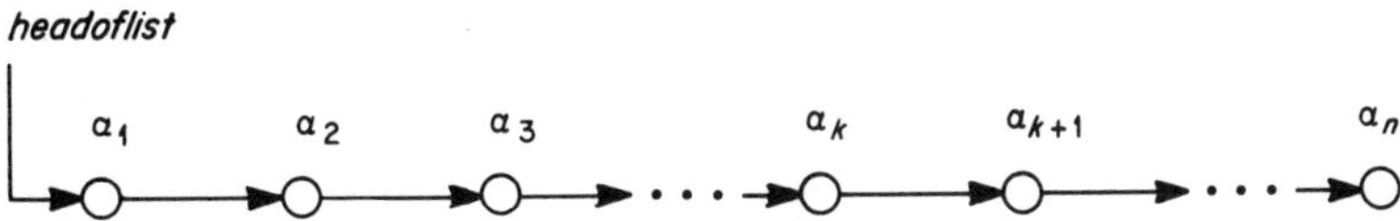

& (the contents of records $\alpha_{k+1}, \ldots, \alpha_n$ have been printed in reverse order).

One step of the loop will consist in finding α_k and writing contents (α_k). The three programs differ essentially in how they discover α_k.

2.3.1. *PL*1

We use a stack of *pointer*(element), manipulated with the help of the condition '*emptystack*' and two primitives:

push(*expr*): place the value of the expression *expr* at the top of the stack.

pop(x): if $\neg$ emptystack then (remove the value at the top of the stack and assign it to variable x) else undefined.

Program *PL*1 has two loops:

(a) The invariant of the first loop can be pictured as follows:

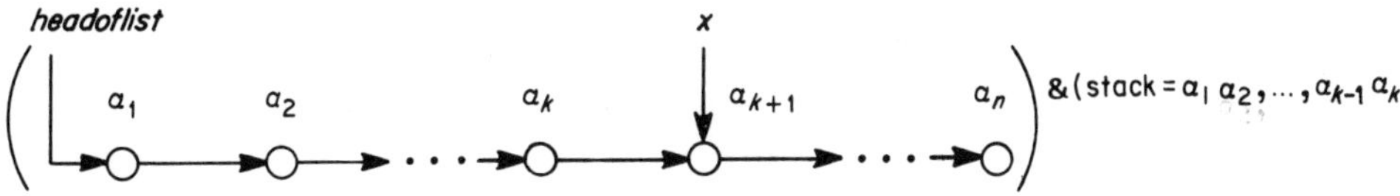

(b) The invariant of the second loop as follows:

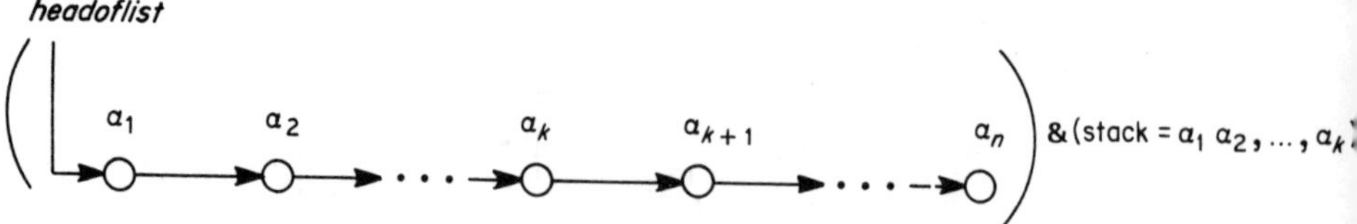

& (the contents of records $\alpha_{k+1}, \ldots, \alpha_n$ have been printed in reverse order).

Remark
The stack has been written with its top to the right.
(c) Program:

```
PL1 : x := headoflist ;
      while tail(x) ≠ nil do
      begin push(x) ; x := tail(x) end;
      write (contents(x)) ;
      while ¬ emptystack do
      begin pop(x) ; write (contents(x)) end
```

(d) Analysis:
If the running time of the primitives *push* and *pop* is constant, then the running time of *PL*1 is of order n (the number of elements in the list). The storage space required, over and above that of the list itself, is also of order n (since the maximum size of the stack is $n-1$).

2.3.2. *PL2*

Program *PL*2 is characterized by the fact that it modifies the list while it is being executed, but at the end of execution the list reappears in its original form.

Like *PL*1, it has two loops.

(a) Invariant of the first loop. This invariant Inv1 can be pictured as follows:

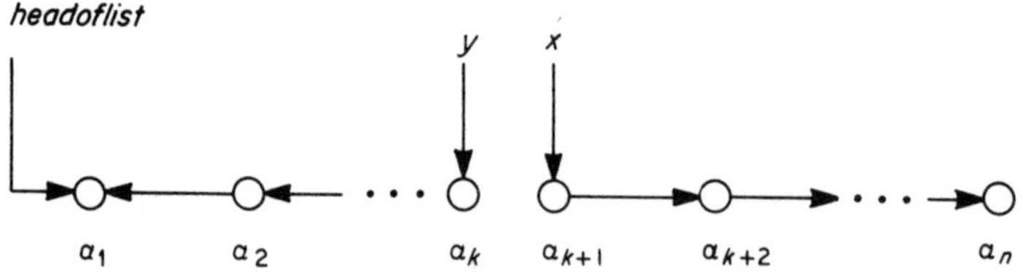

where x stands for any one of the elements in the list (if x stands for α_1, we suppose $y = nil$).

(b) Invariant of the second loop:
Inv1 & (the contents of the records $\alpha_{k+1}, \ldots, \alpha_n$ have been printed in reverse order).

(c) Program:

```
PL2 : y : = nil ; x := headoflist;
      while tail(x) ≠ nil do
      begin z := tail(x) ; tail(x) := y ; y:=x ; x:=z end;
      write (contents(x)) ;
      while y ≠ nil do
      begin z:=x ; x:=y ; y:=tail(x) ; tail(x):=z ;
            write(contents(x))
      end
```

(d) Analysis
The running time is of order n and the storage space required, over and above that of the list itself, is a constant which does not depend on the length of the list.

2.3.3. *PL3*

To find element α_k of the list when $\alpha_{k+1}, \ldots, \alpha_n$ have already been printed, program *PL3* uses an integer variable c whose value is k; α_k can then be determined by a search starting from the head of the list. *PL3* has three loops:
(a) First loop: computation of the initial value of c, namely $n-1$
(b) Invariant of the second loop:

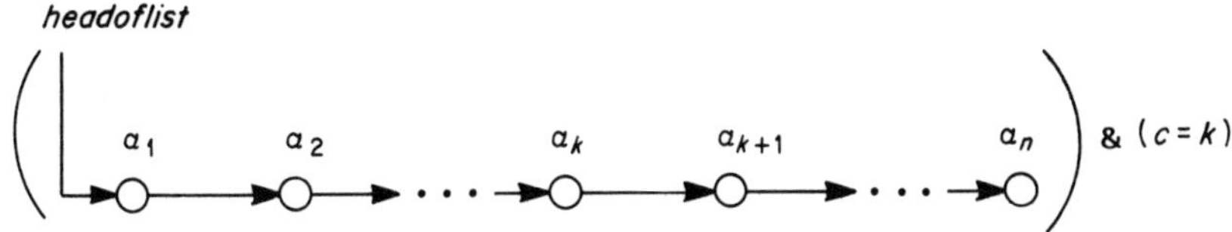

& (the contents of the records $\alpha_{k+1}, \ldots, \alpha_n$ have been printed in reverse order).

The third loop is embedded in the second and allows us to find α_k by a search starting from the *headoflist*.
(c) Program:

```
       PL3 :  c:=0; x := headoflist;
(1)           while tail(x) ≠ nil do
              begin c:=c+1 ; x:=tail(x) end;
              write(contents(x));
              comment: the invariant of the second loop is true,
                       with c = n−1;
(2)           while c ≠ 0 do
              begin c := c−1 ; x := headoflist ;
(3)             for i := 1 step 1 to c do x:= tail(x) ;
                write (contents(x))
              end
```

(d) Analysis

The storage space used over and above that of the list itself is a constant which does not depend on the number n of elements in the list.

The number of traversals of loops (1) and (2) is $n-1$.

number of executions of loop (3) on 1st traversal of loop (2) is $n-2$
on 2nd $n-3$

$\vdots$ $\vdots$

number of executions of loop (3) on ith traversal of loop (2) is $n-i-1$

$\vdots$ $\vdots$

The number of executions of loop (3) is therefore

$$\sum_{i=1}^{n-1} (n-i-1) = \frac{(n-1)(n-2)}{2}.$$

The running time of $PL3$ is therefore of the form $K_1n^2 + K_2n + K_3$, where K_1, K_2 and K_3 are constants independent of n. The running time is therefore of order n^2.

Summary

Program	Characteristics		
	Time	Space	Modification of list during execution
$PL1$	n	n	no
$PL2$	n	constant	yes
$PL3$	n	constant	no

2.4. Logarithmic reduction

Consider an algorithm whose running time is of order $f(n)$ for some function f. We shall use the term *logarithmic reduction* to refer to any optimization procedure which allows us to pass from this algorithm to another algorithm whose running time is order $\log(f(n))$.

2.4.1. Calculating the product of two non-negative integers

An immediate algorithm for calculating the product of two non-negative integers A and B consists in adding value A exactly B times to an accumulator initialized to 0. To program this algorithm, we can use two variables a and b

initialized to A and B respectively, a variable z which plays the role of the accumulator and a loop with invariant $z + ab = AB$, terminating for $b = 0$. This gives the following program:

```
M : z := 0 ;
    while b > 0 do
    begin
      z := z+a ;
      b := b-1
    end
```

The loop is executed B times and on termination we have $z = AB$.

Now suppose we are given the following three primitives, which can be applied to an integer value x:

'division by 2'	denoted by x **div** 2
'multiplication by 2'	denoted by x * 2
'evenness'	denoted by $even(x)$

(These three primitives correspond, in a binary representation of integers, to the operations: shift right, shift left and test whether the rightmost bit is set.)

How can we write an equivalent program, i.e. one which calculates the same function, but whose running time is order (log B)?

The answer is that we modify the loop of program M in such a way as to execute $b := b$ **div** 2 instead of $b := b-1$, while keeping the invariant $z + ab = AB$ and the loop condition $b = 0$ the same.

The instructions which make up this loop will change the variables a,b and z. We shall begin by writing a program in which the values of these variables are saved at the start of the body of the loop, with the help of additional variables $a1$, $b1$, and $z1$. The sequence of instructions P to be defined is then such that:

$(z + ab = AB)\ \{a1 := a\ ;\ b1 := b\ ;\ z1 := z\ ;\ P\}\ (z + ab = AB)$

It is obvious that:

$(z + ab = AB)\ \{a1 := a\ ;\ b1 := b\ ;\ z1 := z\}\ (z1 + a1.b1 = AB)$

All that is required therefore is that P should satisfy:

$(z1 + a1.b1 = AB)\ \{P\}\ (z + ab = AB)$

Let us suppose that P is of the form $a := \alpha$; $b := b1$ **div** 2 ; $z := \zeta$, where α and ζ are expressions which do not contain either a or b or z (so that the order of these assignments is irrelevant). The above statement will then be true if α and ζ satisfy the following equation (obtained by applying the assignment axiom):

$$\zeta + \alpha \left\lfloor \frac{b1}{2} \right\rfloor = z1 + a1.b1$$

The solution to this equation depends on whether or not $b1$ is even. If $b1$ is

even, an obvious solution is $(\alpha\ \zeta) = (a1 * 2, z1)$
If $b1$ is odd, we find $\zeta + \alpha/2\,(b1 - 1) = z1 + a1.b1$

$$(\zeta - \alpha/2) + \alpha/2\ b1 = z1 + a1.b1$$

so that $(\alpha, \zeta) = (a1 * 2,\ z1 + a1)$
The solution for α being the same in both cases, we obtain the following program:

```
M2:   z := 0 ;
      while b > 0 do
      begin a1 := a ; b1 := b ; z1 := z ;
            a := a1 * 2 ;
            b := b1 div 2 ;
            z := if even(b1) then z1 else z1 + a1
      end
```

Now let us discuss the introduction of variables $a1$, $b1$, and $z1$.

(a) As variable $z1$ appears only in the expression ζ, there is clearly no point in saving the value of z. On the other hand, variables $a1$ and $b1$ are necessary: their value is used in ζ. So we obtain:

```
M3:   z := 0 ;
      while b > 0 do
      begin a1 := a ; b1 := b ;
            a := a1 * 2 ;
            b := b1 div 2 ;
            if ¬ even(b1) then z := z + a1
      end
```

(b) The value of $a1$ in the assignment $z := z + a1$ can be discovered without explicitly saving it. Indeed, following the execution of $a := a1 * 2$, we have $a = 2.a1$, whence $a1 = a/2$. So we get to:

```
M4:   z := 0 ;
      while b > 0 do
      begin b1 := b ;
            a := a * 2 ;
            b := b1 div 2 ;
            if ¬ even(b1) then z := z + (a div 2)
      end
```

Exercise
Why does the same argument not apply to $b1$?

(c) Finally, by changing the order of assignments to a, b and z in $M3$, we no longer have to use $a1$ and $b1$.

```
M5:   z := 0 ;
      while b > 0 do
      begin if ¬ even(b) then z := z + a ;
            a := a * 2 ;
            b := b div 2
      end
```

Exercises

(1) Apply to program M a logarithmic reduction to base 10 to find the classical multiplication algorithm of two integers.

(2) Obtain by logarithmic reduction an algorithm for calculating A^B (A and B positive integers) from an algorithm for exponentiation by successive multiplications.

(3) Take an operation $\otimes$ between integers, defined by:

$a \otimes 0 = 1$

$a \otimes b = a^{a \otimes (b-1)}$

It is easy to write a program for calculating $a \otimes b$, analogous to program M, using a primitive for 'exponentiation'. Why does the procedure of logarithmic reduction used for multiplication and exponentiation (exercise 2) not apply to this algorithm?

2.4.2. Finding an element in an ordered array

Given:

— an array L of N elements with indices 1 to N, such that $L(i) < L(i+1)$ for $i = 1, 2, \ldots, N-1$

— a value A,

the problem is to discover:

if A occurs in the array, the index i such that $A = L(i)$ or, if A does not occur in L, the index i of the element immediately preceding A (if $A < L(1)$, one can take $i = 0$).

2.4.2.1. *Sequential search*

A simple algorithm consists of running through array L sequentially, by a loop with invariant $L(i) \leqslant A < L(N)$ and termination condition $A < L(i+1)$.

Observing that cases $A \geqslant L(N)$ and $A < L(1)$ are incompatible with the chosen invariant, we obtain the following program:

```
SS:     if a ≥ L(n) then i := n
        else if a < L(1) then i := 0
           else begin i := 1;
                      while a ≥ L(i+1) do i := i+1
                 end ;
        present : = if i=0 then
                      false
                      else if a = L(i) then
                      true
                      else false
```

Analysis

The running time of program *SS* will obviously depend on the value $ind(A)$ of the index we are looking for. There are $N+1$ possible values for $ind(A)$. Leaving aside the special cases $ind(A) = 0$ and $ind(A) = N$ (where the loop is not executed), consider the case where $1 \leqslant ind(A) \leqslant N-1$. The loop is then executed $ind(A)-1$ times. Depending on the value of A, it can therefore be executed 0, 1, 2, . . . or $N-2$ times.

It is also interesting to have an analysis of the *average* number of executions of the loop, that is to say of the average value of the numbers 0, 1, 2, . . . , $N-2$ weighted according to their probability of occurrence. This will depend on the distribution of the inputs.

Let $P(i)$ be the probability that $ind(A) = i$, depending on the distribution function of A and the elements of array L.

The average number of executions of the loop is then:

$$n_m = \sum_{i=1}^{N-1} (i-1)\, P(i)$$

If the $N+1$ values of ind(A) are *equiprobable*, then $P(i) = \dfrac{1}{N+1}$, and we obtain:

$$n_m = \frac{(N-1)(N-2)}{2(N+1)}$$

In this case, the average execution time of *SS* is order N.

Exercise

Show that if each of the cases $ind(A) = 0$ and $ind(A) = N$ has probability q, and every other case probability p, it follows that:

$$n_m = \frac{N-2}{2}(1 - 2q)$$

2.4.2.2. *Binary Search*

In the worst case, the loop of program *SS* is executed $(N-2)$ times and so has a running time of order N. How can one find an equivalent program whose running time is order $(\log N)$ in the worst case?

As in section 2.4.1, it is a case of reducing the number of executions of the loop. In the multiplication program M, variable b is initialized to B, and decreased by 1 at each step until $b = 0$. It therefore assumes all values from B to 0. The logarithmic reduction consists in assigning to b, at each step, the value $\lfloor b/2 \rfloor$, that is to say, the median value of the interval $[0,b]$. In the case of SS, the variable i, initially 1, assumes in succession all values from 1 to ind(A). The task here is not so simple since $ind(A)$ is unknown; in the worst case, $ind(A) = N-1$.

By assigning to i at each step the value $\lfloor (i+N)/2 \rfloor$, the median value of the interval $[i,N]$, one can apply a similar procedure to that described in 2.4.1. If $ind(A) = N-1$, the invariant $L(i) \leqslant A < L(N)$ is maintained and a logarithmic reduction is thereby achieved. But of course, this invariant is not maintained in general: for a median value J, one can obtain $A < L(J)$, which prevents the assignment of the value J to i. One is thus led to introduce a new variable s, initialized to N, and to use the invariant:

$$L(i) \leqslant A < L(s)$$

maintained in the case $A < L(J)$ through the assignment of J to s.
The body of the loop then becomes:

```
j := (i+s) div 2 ;
if a < L(j) then s := j else i := j
```

Analysis

In order to analyse the program, consider the successive values of the expression $s-i$. Suppose initially that N has the form 2^K+1. The value of $s-i$ before the execution of the loop is then 2^K, and it is easy to verify that the instructions of the loop have the effect, at each step, of changing the value $s-i$ into $\lfloor (s-i)/2 \rfloor$. The final value of $s-i$ is greater than or equal to 1. The number of executions of the loop is therefore less than or equal to K.

In the general case, let K be such that $2^{K-1}+1 \leqslant N < 2^K+1$ (or equivalently, $K-1 < \log_2 N \leqslant K$). It follows from this that the number of executions of the loop is less than or equal to K. Hence the running time is order $(\log N)$, in the worst case.

The program thus obtained can be improved by observing that in the body of the loop, i is not modified if a is strictly less than $L(j)$. It is therefore pointless to recompute the condition $a \geqslant L(i+1)$. This gives:

```
BS:  if a ≥ L(n) then i := n
     else   if a < L(1) then i := 0
            else
            begin i := 1 ; s := n ;
               while a ≥ L(i+1) do
               begin j := (i+s) div 2 ;
                  while a < L(j) do
                  begin s := j ; j := (i+s) div 2 end ;
                  i := j
               end
            end ;
     present := if i=0 then
                false
                else if a=L(i) then
                true
                else false
```

Exercise

Compare this program with a binary search program where the termination condition of the loop is $s = i+1$.

Conclusion

It can be shown that program *BS* has an average running time of order (log *N*). This marks an improvement on the average time calculated in the last section for program *SS*. For certain values of *A*, it is, however, obvious that program *SS* is faster than program *BS*.

2.4.3. Calculating the integer square root of a non-negative integer

2.4.3.1 The aim in this section is to obtain a program for extracting the square root of an integer $A \geqslant 0$, whose running time is of order (log $\lfloor\sqrt{A}\rfloor$). By definition, x is the integer square root of A if $x^2 \leqslant A < (x+1)^2$. From this, the following program $R1$ can be derived immediately, using a loop invariant $0 \leqslant x^2 \leqslant A$. Its running time is order $\lfloor\sqrt{A}\rfloor$ (the variable a is initialized to A).

```
R1 : x := 0 ;
     while (x + 1) ↑ 2 ≤ a do x := x+1
```

Note the similarity between this program and program *SS* in the last section. However, in $R1$, there is no given bound to the interval traversed by the values of x.

If some variable d can be initialized to a value strictly greater than $\lfloor\sqrt{A}\rfloor$, we can follow a similar procedure to the one which led to binary search (§ 2.4.2.2).

We choose the invariant $x \leqslant \lfloor\sqrt{A}\rfloor < d$ (satisfied for $x = 0$ and $d > \lfloor\sqrt{A}\rfloor$).

The logarithmic reduction will consist in assigning to x or d the median value $\lfloor(x+d)/2\rfloor$. The termination condition of the loop is $d-x = 1$.

The following program is obtained:

```
R2 : x := 0 ;
     while d−x > 1 do
     begin j := (x+d) div 2 ;
        if j ↑ 2 > a then d := j else x := j
     end
```

Now let us examine the problem of finding the initial value of d. This value can be arbitrary, provided one has $d > \lfloor \sqrt{A} \rfloor$.

The initialization of d must have a running time of order $\leqslant \log(\lfloor \sqrt{A} \rfloor)$. We can choose 2^K as the initial value of d, provided K is such that: $2^{K-1} \leqslant \lfloor \sqrt{A} \rfloor < 2^K$. Hence the initialization:

```
d := 1 ;
while d ↑ 2 ≤ a do d := d * 2
```

What for binary search was a particular case (considered in the analysis) becomes for $R2$ *the general case*: the expression $d-x$ takes on successive values the powers of 2. This suggests modifying program $R2$ so that the variable is no longer d (the upper limit of the interval) but $l = d-x$ (the length of the interval).

The loop invariant used is then $x \leqslant \lfloor \sqrt{A} \rfloor < x+l$. The value of l being a power of 2, the median value of the interval is $x + l/2$, and the length becomes $l/2$.

The body of the loop therefore becomes:

```
j := x + l div 2 ;
if j ↑ 2 ≤ a then x := j ;
l := l div 2
```

This can be written more simply:

```
l := l div 2 ;
if (x+l) ↑ 2 ≤ a then x := x+l
```

and gives the following program:

```
R3 : x := 0 ;
     l := 1 ; while l ↑ 2 ≤ a do l := l * 2 ;
     while l > 1 do
     begin l := l div 2 ;
        if (x+l) ↑ 2 ≤ a then x := x+l
     end
```

2.4.3.2 Is it possible to achieve the logarithmic reduction just described by only using the arithmetic primitives +, −, ∗2, **div** 2 (cf. § 2.4.1)? To do this, we will have to eliminate the expressions $l \uparrow 2$ and $(x+l) \uparrow 2$ in program $R3$, that is to say, change the variables so that these computations can be expressed in different terms.

We can decide, for example, to introduce three variables u, y and z, such that:

> the condition $(u = l^2)$ is an invariant of the first loop of $R3$; the condition C, $(u = l^2)$ & $(y = a-x^2)$ & $(z = l^2 + 2\times l)$, is an invariant of the second loop of $R3$, and is true after the instruction $l := l$ **div** 2 of this loop.

It is easy to verify that:

$$(u = l^2) \,\&\, (l^2 \leqslant a) \sim (u \leqslant a)$$

and $$C \,\&\, ((x+l)^2 \leqslant a) \sim C \,\&\, (z \leqslant y)$$

This means that it is no longer necessary to compute either l^2, or $(x+l)^2$.

We still have to modify program $R3$ if we are to satisfy our hypothesis about predicate C.

(a) We have:

$$(u = l^2) \,\&\, (y = a-(x+l)^2) \,\&\, (z = l^2 + 2l(x+l)) \; \{x := x+l\} C$$
$$(u = l^2) \,\&\, (y=a-x - (2xl+l^2)) \,\&\, (z = l^2 + 2xl + 2l^2) \; \{x := x+l\} C \qquad (1)$$

Our aim is to re-establish C as precondition. We can adopt the same procedure as in section 2.4.1, and introduce variables $u1$, $y1$ and $z1$; a similar line of reasoning leads us to the following conclusion:

$$C\{y := y - z \; ; \; z := z + u * 2 \; ; \; x := x+l\} C \qquad (2)$$

Note that this solution can also be reached intuitively from (1). Then all we have to do is to verify that (2) is true.

(b) On the other hand, we have:

$$\left(u = \left\lfloor \frac{l}{2} \right\rfloor\right) \,\&\, (y = a-x) \,\&\, \left(z = \left\lfloor \frac{l}{2} \right\rfloor + 2x \left\lfloor \frac{l}{2} \right\rfloor\right) \; \{l := l \textbf{ div } 2\} \; C$$

and we have to re-establish precondition C & $(l > 1)$.

We have seen that l always has a value to the power of 2; hence

$$(l > 1) \rightarrow \left(\left\lfloor \frac{l}{2} \right\rfloor = \frac{l}{2}\right).$$

Thus we have:

$$(l > 1) \,\&\, \left(u = \frac{l^2}{4}\right) \,\&\, (y = a-x^2) \,\&\, \left(z = \frac{l^2}{4} + xl\right) \; \{l := l \; div \; 2\} \; C$$

The same procedure as before leads to:

$$C \,\&\, (l > 1) \; \{u := u \textbf{ div } 4 \; ; \; z := z \textbf{ div } 2 - u \; ; \; l := l \textbf{ div } 2\} \; C$$

Remark
To simplify writing the program, X **div** 4 will denote the operation (x **div** 2) **div** 2, and $x * 4$ the operation $((x * 2) * 2$.

(c) Finally, we have:
$(u = 4l^2)\ \{l := l * 2\}\ (u = l^2)$
and: $(u = l^2)\ \{u := u * 4\ ;\ l := l * 2\}\ (u = l^2)$.

Not forgetting that we need to initialize u, y, and z, we obtain the following program:

```
R4 :  x := 0 ;
      l := 1 ; u := 1 ;
      while u ≤ a do begin u := u * 4 ; l := l * 2 end ;
      y := a ; z := u ;
      while l > 1 do
      begin   u := u div 4 ; z := z div 2 − u ;
              l := l div 2 ;
              if z ≤ y then
              begin y := y − z ; z := z + u * 2 ;
                    x := x + l
              end
      end
```

To conclude, notice that variable x has ceased to be useful. Its final value, obtained when $l = 1$, can be determined from the final value of z by the relation $z = 2x + 1$, and can be written $x = \lfloor z/2 \rfloor$. We can therefore dispense with the instructions $x := 0$ and $x := x+l$. So it appears that variable l has also ceased to be useful, since the condition $l > 1$ is equivalent to $u > 1$ ($l > 0$ being an invariant of the second loop). Finally we obtain the following program:

```
R5 :  u := 1;
      while u ≤ a do u := u * 4 ;
      y := a ; z := u ;
      while u > 1 do
      begin u := u div 4 ; z div 2 − u ;
            if z ≤ y then
            begin y := y − z ; z := z + u  end
      end ;
      x := z div 2
```

Exercise
Attempt a transformation of program $R3$ by introducing three variables u, v, and y such that the assertion $(u = l^2)\ \&\ (v = xl)\ \&\ (y = a-x^2)$ is invariant in the second loop.

Compare this with the classical algorithm for extracting square roots.

Comments and Bibliography

The simultaneous construction of a program and its proof has been advocated by Dijkstra. Numerous examples can be found in his book (Dijkstra, 1976) and in his articles, in particular the calculation of GCD, the problem of the three-coloured flag, and logarithmic reductions. Section 2.4 on logarithmic reductions gives examples of program transformations: the starting point is a correct but inefficient program which is then modified in a series of steps aimed at finding an efficient program. Other program transformations can be seen in Chapter 6. Examples of the systematic construction of programs are discussed in the following works: Wirth, 1976; Gerbier, 1977; Alagic and Arbib, 1978; Meyer and Baudoin, 1978; Gries, 1981; Arsac, 1983; Mahl and Boussard, 1983. For a discussion of programming methods, consult Pair's article (Pair, 1978).

Chapter 3

Proof and Analysis of Iterative Programs—Further Material

In this chapter we present:

The concepts of the weakest precondition and strongest postcondition of a sequence of instructions (§3.1);
A study of different types of axioms for assignment (§3.2);
Axioms and rules of deduction for certain constructions in programming languages (blocks, procedures) not studied in Chapter 1 (§3.3 and §3.4);
Further material on the analysis of programs (§3.5).

3.1. Weakest precondition and strongest postcondition of a sequence of instructions

We have used (in sections 1.3 and 1.4) the notation W_E to describe the set of values of variables of a program satisfying a condition E, and the notation f_P to describe the function calculated by a sequence of instructions P. If the function f_P is defined for all values in W_E, then P does not loop or execute an undefined operation (division by zero, for example) as long as the precondition E is satisfied. We denote this property by $term_E P$.

Consider now a statement $E\{P\}S$. We have the following properties:

(i) $E\{P\}S$ is true if and only if $f_P(W_E) \subseteq W_S$
(ii) if $term_E P$ then:
$E\{P\}S$ is true if and only if $W_E \subseteq f_P^{-1}(W_S)$

Examples

(1) Consider the statement $(q > 0)\ \{q := q+1\}\ (q > 0)$, where q is the only variable of the program. We have:
$W_E = W_S = \mathbb{N}^+$,
$f_{q\ :=\ q+1}(\mathbb{N}^+) = \mathbb{N}^+ - \{1\} \subseteq \mathbb{N}^+$,
and $\mathbb{N}^+ \subseteq f^{-1}_{q:=\ q+1}(\mathbb{N}^+) = \mathbb{N}$.
(2) Consider the statement
$(q \geqslant 0)\ \&\ (y \geqslant 0)\ \{q := q\ \mathbf{div}\ y\}\ (q \geqslant 0)\ \&\ (y \geqslant 0)$,
where q and y are the only variables of the program.

We have: $W_E = W_S = \mathbb{N} \times \mathbb{N}$,

$$f_{q:=q \textbf{ div } y}(\mathbb{N} \times \mathbb{N}) = \mathbb{N} \times \mathbb{N}^+ \subset W_S,$$

but $f^{-1}_{q:=q \textbf{ div } y}(\mathbb{N} \times \mathbb{N}) = \mathbb{N} \times \mathbb{N}^+ \supseteq W_E$.

In the case $W_E = f_P^{-1}(W_S)$, E is *the weakest precondition* which has to be satisfied before execution of P in order for S to hold afterwards. Indeed, if $E'\{P\}S$ and $\text{term}_{E'}P$ then $W_{E'} \subseteq f_P^{-1}(W_S) = W_E$, and so $E' \rightarrow E$.

On the other hand, if $f_P(W_E) = W_S$, S is *the strongest postcondition* which is satisfied after execution of P provided E holds beforehand.

Indeed, if $E\{P\}S'$ then $f_P(W_E) = W_S \subseteq W_{S'}$, and so $S \rightarrow S'$. We denote by *wp* the function which, for a given sequence of instructions and a given postcondition, returns the corresponding weakest precondition, and by *sp* the function which, for a given precondition and sequence of instructions, returns the corresponding strongest postcondition.
(*Remark*: $wp(P,S)$ and $sp(E,P)$ are defined up to equivalence only.)

We now give two properties of the functions *wp* and *sp*.

3.1.1. Proposition

For all conditions S and all sequences of instructions P,

$$sp(wp(P, S), P) \rightarrow S.$$

Proof
Suppose $E \sim wp(P, S)$. Then $W_E = f_P^{-1}(W_S)$, which implies

$$f_P(W_E) = f_P(f_P^{-1}(W_S)) \subseteq W_S$$

or, in terms of predicates: $E \sim wp(P, S)$ implies $sp(E, P) \rightarrow S$.

3.1.2. Proposition

For all conditions E and all sequences of instructions P, if $term_E P$, then $E \rightarrow wp(P,sp(E, P))$.

Proof
Suppose $S \sim sp(E, P)$. Then $W_S = f_P(W_E)$. It follows that

$$f_P^{-1}(W_S) = f_P^{-1}(f_P(W_E)) \supseteq W_E$$

In terms of predicates, this gives

$$S \sim sp(E, P) \text{ implies } E \rightarrow wp(P, S).$$

Exercise
Given a condition E and a sequence of instructions P, what conditions must f_P satisfy for it to be the case that $E \sim wp(P, sp(E, P))$?

3.1.3. Using weakest preconditions and strongest postconditions in proofs

3.1.3.1. *Weakest preconditions*

It follows from the definition of *wp* that for all conditions E and S, and all sequences of instructions P:

$$(E\{P\}S \;\&\; term_E P) \sim (E \rightarrow wp(P, S)).$$

In particular,

$$term_E P \sim (E \rightarrow wp(P, \text{true})).$$

This corresponds to the fact that the set of values which satisfy $wp(P, \text{true})$ is just the domain of definition of function f_P (that is to say the set of values for which program P gives a result). We can therefore use $wp(P, S)$ to prove the *total* correctness of programs.

A system for proving total correctness using weakest preconditions will involve:

(a) Axioms which, for each primitive instruction, give the weakest precondition associated with a given postcondition. For assignment, the axioms given in Chapter 1 generally play this role (see §3.2.1).
(b) Deduction rules which permit the construction of the weakest precondition of a non-primitive instruction P from the weakest preconditions of the instructions which constitute P.

Example
Suppose we wish to determine $wp($ **if** B **then** P **else** $Q, S)$. If evaluation of B gives a result, then:

$$wp(\textbf{if } B \textbf{ then } P \textbf{ else } Q, S) \sim (B \;\&\; wp(P, S) \vee (\neg B \;\&\; wp(Q, S))$$

Now, evaluation of B gives a result if and only if

wp (**if** B **then**, true) is true. Hence, in the general case:
wp (**if** B **then** P **else** Q, S)
$\sim$ if $wp($**if** B **then**, true)
then $(B \;\&\; wp(P, S)) \vee (\neg B \;\&\; wp(Q, S))$
else false

There is no such simple rule for the while loop.

The complexity of the rules for determining the weakest precondition of a while loop can be illustrated by the following known facts:

The problem of determining whether an arbitrary while loop terminates is undecidable. As a result, the condition $wp($**while** B **do** P, true) is not computable for every B and P.

The resolution of certain well known problems in Number Theory is equivalent to proving the termination of some program.
For example, we do not know whether
wp(**while** $n \neq 1$ **do**
    $n :=$ **if** *even*(n) **then** n **div** 2
        else $3*n+1$, true) ~ ($n \geqslant 1$).
This is Collatz's conjecture.

Remark
The axioms and deduction rules of Chapter 1 allow us to prove statements of the form $E\{P\}S$, where $E \nrightarrow wp(P, S)$. For instance, we have proved in section 1.2.4 that

$$(a \geqslant 0)\ \{Div\}\ (a = bq+r)\ \&\ (q \geqslant 0)\ \&\ (0 \leqslant r < b).$$

This is in no way contradictory, since we were there dealing with proofs of partial correctness.

3.1.3.2. *Strongest postconditions*

It follows from the definition of *sp* that

$$E\{P\}S \sim (sp(E, P) \rightarrow S).$$

A proof system based on strongest postconditions would thus allow us to carry out proofs of *partial* correctness.

The corresponding axioms for assignment can be found in section 3.2.2. For the conditional instruction, a deduction rule is given by the property:

$$sp(E, \textbf{if } B \textbf{ then } P \textbf{ else } Q) \sim sp(E\&B, P) \vee sp(E\&\neg B, Q)$$

on the assumption that evaluation of B always gives a result. In the general case:

sp(E, **if** B **then** P **else** Q)
~ *sp* (E&(if *wp*(**if** B **then**, true) then B else false), P)
$\vee$ *sp*(E&(if *wp*(**if** B **then**, true) then $\neg B$ else false), Q)

3.2. Assignment axioms

3.2.1. Weakest precondition and strongest postcondition for an assignment axiom

A precondition E, calculated according to the rule given in Chapter 1 for the formation of assignment axioms, will be the weakest precondition of an assignment $x :=$ *expr* and a postcondition S, whenever $term_E(x{:=}expr)$ is true.

In this case, the axiom can be written

$$wp(x := expr, S)\ \{x := expr\}\ S.$$

In the general case, we have:

$$wp(x := expr, S) \sim \text{if } wp(x := expr, \text{true}) \text{ then } S(x/expr) \text{ else false.}$$

The condition $wp(x := expr, \text{true})$ states that:

> x and the operands in *expr* are defined (e.g. array indices are between bounds, pointers which reference variables are different from *nil*, etc. . . .); all the effective operations give a result (e.g. compatibility between different types of operands, no division by zero, etc. . . .)

This does not invalidate the axioms for partial correctness given in Chapter 1 because if $term_E(x := expr)$ is false, then the statement $E\ \{x := expr\}\ S$ is true. The precondition of these axioms may nevertheless be reinforced by conditions implied by $wp(x := expr, \text{true})$.

For example, if m and n are the bounds of an array a, then instead of

$$(y > 0)\ \{x := a(j)\}\ (y > 0)$$

and

$$(a(j) = y)\ \{x := a(j)\}\ (x = y)$$

one can use

$$(m \leqslant j \leqslant n)\ \&\ (y > 0)\ \{x := a(j)\}\ (y > 0)$$

$$\textbf{if } (m \leqslant j \leqslant n) \textbf{ then } (a(j) = y) \textbf{ else } \mathit{false}\ \{x := a(j)\}\ (x = y).$$

According to proposition 3.1.1, if $E\{x := expr\}S$ is an axiom, S is not necessarily the strongest postcondition associated with E. It follows that assignment axioms cannot in general be written in the form

$$E\{x := expr\}\ sp(E, x := expr).$$

Take, for instance the axiom $\{1/x \geqslant 0)\ \{x := 1/x\}\ (x \geqslant 0)$. We have $(1/x \geqslant 0) \sim (x > 0)$, but $sp(x > 0, x := 1/x) \sim (x > 0)$.

We shall now look at formation rules for axioms from precondition to postcondition. Axioms constructed according to these rules can always be written in the form $E\{x := expr\}\ sp(E, x := expr)$, but not in general in the form $wp(x := expr, S)\ \{x := expr\}\ S$ (see proposition 3.1.2).

3.2.2. Rules for calculating the strongest postcondition of an assignment

For an assignment instruction $x := expr$, only the variable x can be modified. So, $f_{x:=expr}$ is a mapping of the set W of values of program variables to itself, which leaves all components unaltered, except the one corresponding to variable x.

We shall denote by $\pi_x f_{x:=expr}$ the projection of $f_{x:=expr}$ to this component.

For example, for the instruction $q := q+1$ of program *Div* (Chapter 1), we have:

$$f_{q:=q+1}(a,b,q,r) = (a,b,q+1,r)$$

and

$$\pi_q f_{q:=q+1}\ (a,b,q,r) = q+1.$$

Similarly, the rule for calculating the precondition, given in §1.2.3.7, will be written:

$$E \sim S(x/\pi_x f_{x:=expr}).$$

We shall now define two rules for calculating the strongest postcondition of an assignment.

3.2.2.1. *Particular case*

If the restriction of $f_{x:=expr}$ to W_E is total and injective, it possesses an inverse function denoted by $f^{-1}_{x:=expr}$. In this case, one can use the following rule for calculating *sp*:

$$sp(E,\ x := expr) \sim E(x/\pi_x f^{-1}_{x:=expr}).$$

In other words, one obtains the strongest postcondition, associated with a precondition E and an assignment $x := expr$, by substituting for each occurrence of x in E a definition of the projection on component x of the inverse function of $f_{x:=expr}$.

This rule for calculating *sp* gives a formation rule for assignment axioms, from precondition to postcondition, which can be expressed as follows:

'$E\{x := expr\}\ E(x/\pi_x f^{-1}_{x:=expr})$ is an axiom'.

The existence of a functional inverse of $f_{x:=expr}$ allows us to recover the value of x before the assignment from the values of the variables afterwards. This problem has already arisen in connection with program transformations for logarithmic reductions (see §2.4.1), and will arise once more in Chapter 6 when we discuss the elimination of recursion.

Examples

$$sp(q \geqslant 0,\ q := q+1) \sim (q-1 \geqslant 0)$$

$$sp(q \geqslant 0,\ q := q*2) \sim \left(\frac{q}{2} \geqslant 0\right)$$

$$sp(q = 0,\ q := q+a) \sim (q-a = 0)$$

The following axioms are obtained:

$$(q \geqslant 0)\ \{q := q+1\}\ (q-1 \geqslant 0)$$

$$(q \geqslant 0)\ \{q := q*2\}\ \left(\frac{q}{2} \geqslant 0\right)$$

$$(q = 0)\ \{q := q+a\}\ (q-a = 0).$$

The rule does not apply in the case of assignments like $q := 0$, or q:=q **div** 2.

Rule 3.2.2.1 allows us to prove programs 'from left to right'. For instance, suppose we have to establish:

$$(x > 0)\ \{x := x*2\}\ (x > 0).$$

By proceeding as in Chapter 1, from the postcondition to the precondition, we obtain the following axiom:

$$(2x > 0)\ \{x := x*2\}\ (x > 0)$$

and the proof is completed by using the precondition rule, since:

$$(x > 0) \rightarrow (2x > 0)$$

By proceeding in the opposite direction, from precondition to postcondition, we obtain:

$$(x > 0)\ \{x := x*2\}\ \left(\frac{x}{2} > 0\right)$$

and this time we complete the proof by using the postcondition rule, since:

$$\left(\frac{x}{2} > 0\right) \rightarrow (x > 0).$$

Remark

All the assignment axioms given in the preceding examples can just as well be obtained from the postcondition, using rule 1.2.3.7, as from the precondition, using rule 3.2.2.1. In all these examples, function $f_{x:=expr} : W \rightarrow W$ is injective.

The following example shows that if $f_{x:=expr} : W \rightarrow W$ is not injective, this possibility does not exist (see proposition and exercise 3.1.2).

Example

The function $f_{x:=x \textbf{ div } 2}$ is total, but not injective, although its restriction to $W_{x=2y}$ is injective.

By applying rule 3.2.2.1, we obtain the following axiom:

$$(x = 2y)\ \{x := x \textbf{ div } 2\}\ (2x = 2y)$$

which is equivalent to:

$$(x = 2y)\ \{x := x \textbf{ div } 2\}\ (x = y).$$

On the other hand, if we begin from the postcondition $(2x = 2y)$ and use rule 1.2.3.7, we obtain:

$\left(2\left\lfloor\frac{x}{2}\right\rfloor = 2y\right)$ $\{x := x \textbf{ div } 2\}$ $(2x = 2y)$, which is equivalent to

$\left(2\left\lfloor\frac{x}{2}\right\rfloor = 2y\right)$ $\{x := x \textbf{ div } 2\}$ $(x = y)$.

3.2.2.2. *General case*

If there is no inverse function of $f_{x:=expr}$, it is not possible to recover the initial value of x from the values of the variables after assignment. If in some program this initial value is needed, then we have to use an auxiliary variable $x1$ and execute $x1 := x$ before the assignment $x := expr$ (see § 2.4.1). If we have to discover condition $sp(E, x := expr)$, we obviously cannot assume that such a variable $x1$ is present in the program. We simply affirm the existence of an initial value x' of x (the other variables remain unchanged). This gives the following rule for calculating $sp(E, x := expr)$:

$$sp(E, x := expr)$$
$$\sim (\exists x', (x = \pi_x f_{x:=expr}(\ldots, x', \ldots)) \;\&\; E(x/x'))$$

We can then deduce the following rule for the formation of assignment axioms, from precondition to postcondition:

> 'E $\{x := expr\}$ $(\exists x', (x = \pi_x f_{x:=expr}\,(\ldots, x', \ldots)) \;\&\; E(x/x'))$ is an axiom'.

Exercise
Verify the above equivalence when $term_E(x := expr)$ is false.

Examples

(1) $(x > 0)$ $\{x := x \textbf{ div } 2\}$ $\left(\exists x', \left(x = \left\lfloor\frac{x'}{2}\right\rfloor\right) \;\&\; (x > 0)\right)$

(2) (x=5) & (y=3)
$\{x := (x+y) \textbf{ div } 2\}$
$\left(\exists x', \left(x = \left\lfloor\frac{x'+y}{2}\right\rfloor\right) \;\&\; (x'=5) \;\&\; (y=3)\right)$
The postcondition is equivalent to $(x=4)$ & $(y=3)$.

(3) $(x > 0)$ $\{x := 5\}$ $(\exists x', (x = 5) \;\&\; (x' > 0))$
The postcondition is equivalent to $(x = 5)$

(4) $(x > 0)$ $\{x := x+1\}$ $(\exists x', (x = x'+1) + (x' > 0))$
The postcondition is equivalent to $(x-1 > 0)$.
It can be seen from this example that if the conditions of 3.2.2.1 are satisfied, the general rule gives an axiom equivalent to that obtained by using the inverse function $f^{-1}_{x:=expr}$.

(5) Suppose we have to prove:

$$(x > 0)\ \{x := x\ \mathbf{div}\ 2\ ;\ x := x+1\}\ (x > 0).$$

Proceeding as in Chapter 1, starting with the postcondition, we obtain:

$$\left(\left\lfloor \frac{x+1}{2} \right\rfloor > 0\right)\ \{x := x\ \mathbf{div}\ 2\ ;\ x := x+1\}\ (x > 0)$$

and we conclude by using the precondition rule, since:

$$(x > 0) \rightarrow \left(\left\lfloor \frac{x+1}{2} \right\rfloor > 0\right).$$

Proceeding from the precondition, by applying rule 3.2.2.2, we obtain the following axiom:

$$(x > 0)\ \{x := x\ \mathbf{div}\ 2\}\ \left(\exists x',\ \left(x = \left\lfloor \frac{x'}{2} \right\rfloor\right)\ \&\ (x' > 0)\right).$$

By applying rule 3.2.2.1, *we obtain*:

$$\left(\exists x',\ \left(x = \left\lfloor \frac{x'}{2} \right\rfloor\right)\ \&\ (x' > 0)\right)$$

$$\{x := x+1\}$$

$$\left(\exists x',\ \left(x-1 = \left\lfloor \frac{x'}{2} \right\rfloor\right)\ \&\ (x' > 0)\right)$$

and we conclude by applying the postcondition rule, since:

$$\left(\exists x',\ \left(x-1 = \left\lfloor \frac{x'}{2} \right\rfloor\right)\ \&\ (x' > 0)\right) \rightarrow (x > 0).$$

3.2.3. Limitations of assignment axioms

3.2.3.1. *Introduction*

The rules for the formation of assignment axioms may be incorrect if the assignment is to a variable which has more than one name. For example, if a and b denote the same variable, the statement

$$(b > 0)\ \{a := 0\}\ (b > 0)$$

is false, and cannot therefore be asserted as an axiom. In such a case, we will say that a and b are *synonyms*: that is to say that every reference to one (in particular every assignment) is also a reference (an assignment) to the other. This situation can arise, even when the possibility of declaring synonyms (offered for instance by the attribute *defined* in PL1) is absent, when we use index variables or variables referenced by pointers, or procedure calls with parameters.

3.2.3.2. *Index variables*

(Note: We limit ourselves to arrays of *one dimension*. Generalization to arrays of more than one dimension does not present any difficulties.)

Given an array a, $a(expr1)$ and $a(expr2)$ are synonyms if *expr*1 and *expr*2 have the same value. For example, the statement

$$(a(j) > 0)\ \{a(i) := 0\}\ (a(j) > 0)$$

is false if $i=j$.

Take an instruction $a(i) := expr$ and a postcondition S. We are going to define a rule for the formation of axioms of the form $E\{a(i) := expr\}\ S$. We shall use the term *embedded* reference (to array a) to refer to an occurrence of a in the index of another occurrence of a: for example, $a(j)$ in $a(k + a(j))$.

3.2.3.2.1. *a(i) contains no embedded reference* (to array a)

Case 1. Condition *S contains no embedded reference* (to a)
We have the following rule [see the axiom for the primitive *swap(i,j)* of the three-coloured flag, given in §2.2.3.1]:

> Let E be the condition obtained from S by substituting the expression *expr* for all occurrences of $a(y)$, such that $y = i$. Then,
> $E\ \{a(i) := expr\}\ S$ is an axiom.

The application of this rule makes it necessary for us:

- either to prove properties like $y = i$, which may turn out to be very difficult, if not impossible,
- or to treat the cases $y = i$ and $y \neq i$ separately.

Example
Take the sequence of instructions:

$$\begin{aligned} P : a(j+1) &:= a(j)\ ; \\ a(j) &:= a(i); \\ a(i) &:= a(j+1) \end{aligned}$$

We have to prove the following statement:

$$(a(i) = y)\ \&\ (a(j) = x)\ \&\ (i \leqslant j)\ \{P\}\ (a(j) = y)\ \&\ (a(i) = x).$$

We have the two axioms:

(1) $(a(j+1) = x)\ \&\ (a(j+1) = y)\ \&\ (i = j)$
$\{a(i) := (j+1)\}$
$(a(j) = y)\ \&\ (a(i) = x)\ \&\ (i = j)$

(2) $(a(j) = y)\ \&\ (a(j+1) = x)\ \&\ (i \neq j)$
$\{a(i) := a(j+1)\}$
$(a(j) = y)\ \&\ (a(i) = x)\ \&\ (i \neq j)$

From the precondition of (1), we construct the axiom:

$(a(j+1) = x = y)$ & $(i = j)$
$\{a(j) := a(i)\}$
$(a(j+1) = x = y)$ & $(i = j)$

and finally:

$(a(j) = x = y)$ & $(i = j)$
$\{a(j+1) := a(j)\}$
$(a(j+1) = x = y)$ & $(i = j)$.

So we have:

(3) $(a(j) = x = y)$ & $(i = j)$
$\{P\}$
$(a(j) = y)$ & $(a(i) = x)$ & $(i = j)$.

From the precondition of (2), we construct the axiom:

$(a(i) = y)$ & $(a(j+1) = x)$ & $(i \neq j)$
$\{a(j) := a(i)\}$
$(a(j) = y)$ & $(a(j+1) = x)$ & $(i \neq j)$

Now, $(i < j) \rightarrow (i \neq j+1)$.

So we have the axiom:

$(a(i) = y)$ & $(a(j) = x)$ & $(i < j)$
$\{a(j+1) := a(j)\}$
$(a(i) = y)$ & $(a(j+1) = x)$ & $(i < j)$.

Since $(i < j) \rightarrow (i \neq j)$, we have:

(4) $(a(i) = y)$ & $(a(j) = x)$ & $(i < j)$
$\{P\}$
$(a(j) = y)$ & $(a(i) = x)$ & $(i \neq j)$

By the 'or' rule, we obtain from (3) and (4):

$(a(i) = y)$ & $(a(j) = x)$ & $((i = j) \vee (i < j))$
$\{P\}$
$(a(j) = y)$ & $(a(i) = x)$

giving finally:

$(a(i) = y)$ & $(a(j) = x)$ & $(i \leqslant j)$
$\{P\}$
$(a(j) = y)$ & $(a(i) = x)$.

Case 2. Condition S *contains embedded references* (to *a*)

In this case, it may be impossible to apply the preceding rule: several occurrences of $a(y)$ for which $y = i$ may be embedded. For example, take the assignment $a(1) := 1$ and the postcondition $(a(a(1)) = 0)$ & $(a(1) = 1)$. It is not possible to substitute 1 for the two occurrences of a in $a(a(1))$. We modify the rule in the following way: in the case of embedded references, we substitute expr for the *outermost* occurrence of a for which the substitution is possible.

Example
For the given assignment and postcondition, we obtain the axiom:

$$(1 = 0) \ \& \ (1 = 1)$$
$$\{a(1) := 1\}$$
$$(a(a(1)) = 0) \ \& \ (a(1) = 1)$$

which is equivalent to:

$$\mathit{false} \ \{a(1) := 1\} \ \mathit{false}.$$

By substituting for the innermost occurrence of a, one would obtain the precondition $(a(1) = 0) \ \& \ (1 = 1)$ and deduce the false statement:

$$(a(1) = 0) \ \{a(1) := 1\} \ \mathit{false}.$$

Exercise
Prove the statement

$$E \ \{i := a(j) \ ; \ a(i) := 0\} \ (a(a(1)) = 0)$$

where E is equivalent to:

$$(a(a(1)) = 0) \ \& \ (a(j) \neq a(1)) \ \& \ (a(j) \neq 1)$$
$$\vee \ (a(j) = a(1)) \ \& \ (a(j) \neq 1)$$
$$\vee \ (a(0) = 0) \ \& \ (a(j) = 1).$$

3.2.3.2.2. *General case.* The rule in the last section can produce false statements if i contains references to array a. Indeed, when i and y are compared, the values of i and y are a function of the values of the variables, before and after execution of the assignment respectively.

Example
The statement $(1 = 1) \ \{a(a(2)) := 1\} \ (a(a(2)) = 1)$ is false. If initially $a(1) = a(2) = 2$, then after the assignment we will have $a(a(2)) = 2$. Substitution has taken place, since $a(2) = a(2)$, but $a(2)$ can be modified by the assignment.

The assignment $a(i) := \mathit{expr}$ is equivalent to the sequence of two instructions $\alpha := i \ ; \ a(\alpha) := \mathit{expr}$, where α is a symbol not appearing in the program. Rule 3.2.3.2.1 can be applied to the assignment $a(\alpha) := \mathit{expr}$, which gives the following rule:

> Given a postcondition S and the assignment $a(i) := \mathit{expr}$, where i contains references to a, first calculate, according to rule 3.2.3.2.1, the precondition associated with S and the assignment $a(\alpha) := \mathit{expr}$, where α is a symbol which does not appear either in S or in i or in expr. Then, to obtain the required precondition, substitute expression i for the symbol α.

Example

Let us look again at the last example.

The postcondition $a(a(2)) = 1$ is equivalent to:

$$(a(a(2)) = 1) \,\&\, (a(2) = \alpha) \,\&\, (\alpha = 2)$$
$$\vee\ (a(a(2)) = 1) \,\&\, (a(2) \neq \alpha) \,\&\, (\alpha = 2)$$
$$\vee\ (a(a(2)) = 1) \,\&\, (a(2) = \alpha) \,\&\, (\alpha \neq 2)$$
$$\vee\ (a(a(2)) = 1) \,\&\, (a(2) \neq \alpha) \,\&\, (\alpha \neq 2).$$

We obtain, as a precondition of $a(\alpha) := 1$

$$(1 = 1) \,\&\, (1 = \alpha) \,\&\, (\alpha = 2)$$
$$\vee\ (a(1) = 1) \,\&\, (1 \neq \alpha) \,\&\, (\alpha = 2)$$
$$\vee\ (1 = 1) \,\&\, (a(2) = \alpha) \,\&\, (\alpha \neq 2)$$
$$\vee\ (a(a(2)) = 1) \,\&\, (a(2) \neq \alpha) \,\&\, (\alpha \neq 2)$$

It follows that

$$(a(1) = 1) \,\&\, (a(2) = 2) \vee (a(2) \neq 2)$$
$$\{a(a(2)) := 1\}$$
$$(a(a(2)) = 1).$$

3.2.3.3. *Variables referenced by pointers*

This case is similar to that of index variables. If a is the field of some record, and p and q two pointers, then $a(p)$ and $a(q)$ are synonyms whenever p and q have the same value.

The various rules of section 3.2.3.2 apply in the same cases.

3.2.3.4. *Example*

Take the sequence of instructions:

$$P : a(a(t)) := a(s) \;;$$
$$a(s) := a(t) \;;$$
$$a(t) := s$$

and the postcondition $a(a(a(t))) = u$.

We are going to calculate precondition E obtained with the help of the rules in section 3.2.3.2. We shall not apply these rules in detail except for the deduction of statement (11) below.

First we obtain:

(1) $(s = u) \,\&\, (s = t)$
$\{a(t) := s\}$
$(a(a(a(t))) = u) \,\&\, (a(a(t)) = t) \,\&\, (a(t) = t)$

(2) $(s = u) \,\&\, (a(s) = t) \,\&\, (s \neq t)$
$\{a(t) := s\}$
$(a(a(a(t))) = u) \,\&\, (a(a(t)) = t) \,\&\, (a(t) \neq t)$

(3) $(a(a(s)) = u) \,\&\, (a(s) \neq t) \,\&\, (s \neq t)$
$\{a(t) := s\}$
$(a(a(a(t))) = u) \,\&\, (a(a(t)) \neq t) \,\&\, (a(t) \neq t)$

From the preconditions of (1), (2), and (3), we prove:

(4) $(s = t = u)\ \{a(s) := a(t)\}\ (s = t = u)$

(5) $(s = u) \& (s \neq t) \& (a(t) = t)$
$\{a(s) := a(t)\}$
$(s = u) \& (s \neq t) \& (a(s) = t)$

(6) $(s \neq t) \& (a(t) \neq t) \& (a(t) = u) \& (a(t) = s)$
$\{a(s) := a(t)\}$
$(s \neq t) \& (a(s) \neq t) \& (a(a(s)) = u) \& (a(s) = s)$

(7) $(s \neq t) \& (a(t) \neq t) \& (a(a(t)) = u) \& (a(t) \neq s)$
$\{a(s) := a(t)\}$
$(s \neq t) \& (a(s) \neq t) \& (a(a(s)) = u) \& (a\ (s) \neq s)$

Finally we have, from the preconditions of (4), (5), and (6):

(8) $(s = t = u)\ \{a(a(t)) := a(s)\}\ (s = t = u)$

(9) $(s = u) \& (s \neq t) \& (a\ (s) = t) \& (a(t) = t)$
$\{a(a(t)) := a(s)\}$
$(s = u) \& (s \neq t) \& (a(t) = t)$

(10) $(s \neq t) \& (a(t) = s = u) \vee (a(s) = s = u) \& (a(t) = t)$
$\{a(a(t)) := a(s)\}$
$(s \neq t) \& (a(t) = s = u)$

(11) $(a(s) \neq t) \& (a(s) \neq s) \& (a(a(s)) = u) \& (a(t) = t)$
$\vee (s \neq t) \& (a(t) \neq t) \& (a(t) \neq s) \& (a(s) = u)$
$\{a(a(t)) := a(s)\}$
$(s \neq t) \& (a(t) \neq t) \& (a(a(t)) = u) \& (a(t) \neq s)$

(See below for the detailed deduction of this statement.)

Finally, by applying the 'or' rule, we obtain:

$E \sim (s = t = u)$
$\vee (s = u) \& (s \neq t) \& (a(s) = t) \& (a(t) = t)$
$\vee (s \neq t) \& (a(t) = s = u)$
$\vee (s \neq t) \& (a(s) = s = u) \& (a(t) = t)$
$\vee (s \neq t) \& (a(t) \neq t) \& (a(t) \neq s) \& (a(s) = u)$
$\vee (a(s) \neq t) \& (a(s) \neq s) \& (a(a(s)) = u) \& (a(t) = t).$

Deduction of statement (11)

Take the assignment $a(\alpha) := a(s)$
and the postcondition

$$S : (s \neq t) \& (a(t) \neq t) \& (a(t) \neq s) \& (a(a(t)) = u).$$

We have $S \sim S \& ((\alpha = t) \vee (\alpha \neq t) \& ((\alpha = a(t)) \vee (\alpha \neq a(t)))$.
By applying rule 3.2.3.2.1, we obtain the precondition:

$$\begin{aligned}&(\alpha = t) \& (\alpha = a(s)) \& (s \neq t) \& (a(s) \neq t) \& (a(s) \neq s) \& (a(s) = u)\\ \vee\ &(\alpha = t) \& (\alpha \neq a(s)) \& (s \neq t) \& (a(s) \neq t) \& (a(s) \neq s) \& (a(a(s)) = u)\\ \vee\ &(\alpha \neq t) \& (\alpha = a(t)) \& (s \neq t) \& (a(t) \neq t) \& (a(t) \neq s) \& (a(s) = u)\\ \vee\ &(\alpha \neq t) \& (\alpha \neq a(t)) \& S.\end{aligned}$$

Now we replace α by $a(t)$, which gives:

$$\begin{aligned} &\text{false} \\ \vee\ &(a(t) = t)\ \&\ (a(t) \neq a(s))\ \&\ (s \neq t)\ \&\ (a(s) \neq t) \\ &\&\ (a(s) \neq s)\ \&\ (a(a(s)) = u) \\ \vee\ &(a(t) \neq t)\ \&\ (s \neq t)\ \&\ (a(t) \neq s)\ \&\ (a(s) = u) \\ \vee\ &\text{false}. \end{aligned}$$

Hence statement (11).

Remark

We have not considered the case where the pointers have the value *nil*: it may then happen that sequence *P* gives no result. As we saw in section 3.2.1, the preconditions obtained can be reinforced to allow the left and right-hand sides of each assignment to be defined. The precondition then obtained is

$$E\ \&\ (s \neq nil)\ \&\ (t \neq nil)\ \&\ (a(t) \neq nil).$$

One can verify that the six 'cases' which appear in precondition E are mutually exclusive, and correspond to the following six schemas (every arrow represents a pointer different from *nil*):

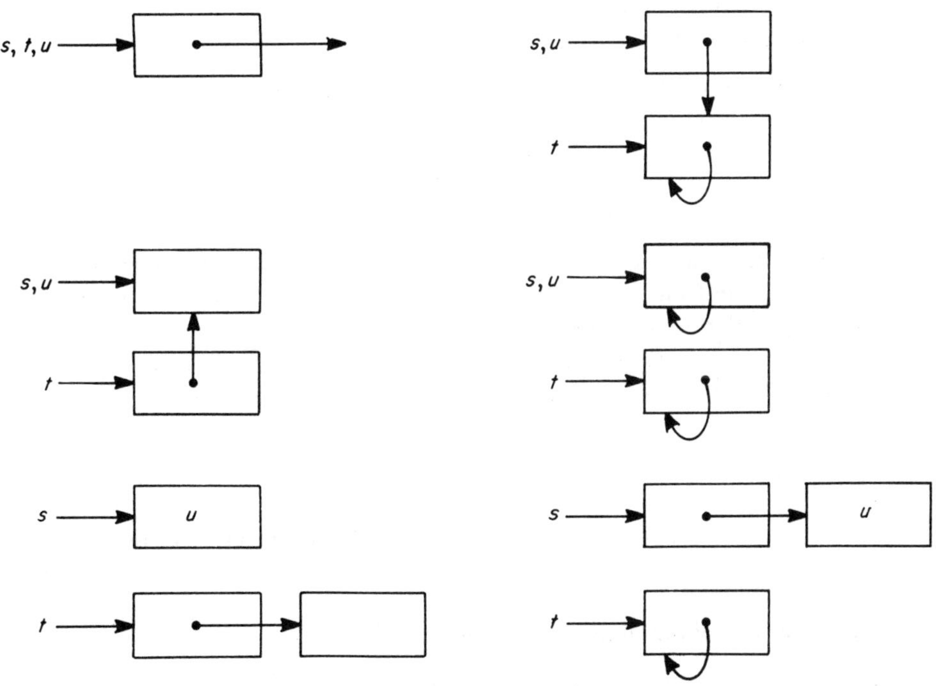

3.2.3.5. *Calls of procedures with parameters*

If, in a procedure call, the actual parameters and the corresponding formal parameters are synonyms, the assignment axioms may not make sense. So the statement $(b > 0)\ \{a := 0\}\ (b > 0)$ is false if

- a is a formal parameter and b the corresponding actual parameter;
- b is a formal parameter and a the corresponding actual parameter;
- a and b are two formal parameters corresponding to the same actual parameter.

Examples

(1) Take the program:

```
begin integer a;
      procedure p (integer x) ; x := a+1 ;
      p(a)
end
```

For the call $p(a)$, x and a are synonyms, and the statement

$$(a+1 = a+1)\ \{x := a+1\}\ (x = a+1)$$

is false.

(2) Take the procedure definition:

procedure r (**integer** x, y) ; $x := y + 1$

For a call such as $r(a,a)$, x and y are synonyms, and the statement

$(y+1 = y+1)\ \{x := y+1\}\ (x = y+1)$

is false.

Remark

Where actual parameters and formal parameters are not synonyms (for instance, if the formal parameters denote variables local to the body of the procedure), the assignment axiom will always make sense.

Restrictions in the use of parameters, so that correct axioms can be produced for procedure calls, will be introduced in section 3.4.

3.3. Further axioms and deduction rules for program proofs

3.3.1. Axiom of the empty instruction

For all conditions E, we have the axiom:

$E\ \{\}\ E.$

3.3.2. Rule for blocks

Consider a block **begin variable** x ; P **end** where '**variable** x' denotes a declaration of a variable x, and P a sequence of instructions. Let P' be a sequence of instructions obtained from P by replacing each occurrence of x by y (where y is not a variable used in P, or in conditions E and S). We then have the following rule:

if E $\{P'\}$ S then E {**begin variable** x ; P **end**} S.

Remark
If the block contains a procedure declaration, x must also be replaced by y in the body of the procedure.

Example
From the statement

$(x < 0)$ & $(u > 0)$ $\{y := 1 ; u := u+y\}$ $(x < 0)$ & $(u > 0)$

we deduce:

$(x < 0)$ & $(u > 0)$
{**begin integer** x ; $x := 1$; $u := u+x$ **end**}
$(x < 0)$ & $(u > 0)$

If the variable x does not appear in conditions E and S, there is no point in introducing y, and the rule is applied with P' identical to P. So, from

$(u > 0)$ $\{x := 1 ; u := u+x\}$ $(u > 0)$

we can deduce:

$(u > 0)$ {**begin integer** x ; $x := 1$; $u := u+x$ **end**} $(u > 0)$.

3.3.3. Rule for 'for' loops

Consider the loop **for** $i := e1$ **step** 1 **to** $e2$ **do** P, in which the sequence of instructions P does not modify the values of $e1$, $e2$ and i, and the expressions $e1$ and $e2$ contain no reference to i. We then have the following rule:

if $(e1 \leqslant i \leqslant e2)$ & E $\{P\}$ $E(i/i+1)$ then $E(i/e1)$
{**for** $i :=$ e1 **step** 1 **to** e2 **do** P}
((e1 > e2) & $E(i/\text{e1})$) $\vee$ ((e1 $\leqslant$ e2) & $E(i/\text{e2}+1)$).

Condition E is an invariant of the *for* loop. We observe that the control variable does not appear either in the precondition or the postcondition of the *for* instruction.

Example
Take the loop **for** $i := 1$ **step** 1 **to** n **do** $T(i) := 0$.
Condition $E : (1 \leqslant \alpha \leqslant i-1) \rightarrow (T(\alpha) = 0)$ is an invariant of the loop.
Indeed:

$E \sim ((1 \leqslant i-1) \rightarrow T(1) = 0) \ \& \ldots \& \ (T(i-1) = 0))$
$E(i/i+1) \sim ((1 \leqslant i) \rightarrow T(1) = 0) \ \& \ldots \& \ T(i) = 0))$
$E(i/i+1) \sim \ ((i = 1) \rightarrow (T(i) = 0))$
$\& \ ((1 \leqslant i-1) \rightarrow (T(1) = 0) \ \& \ldots \& \ (T(i-1) = 0) \ \& \ (T(i) = 0))$

So we have the axiom:

$$((i = 1) \rightarrow (0 = 0))$$
$$\& \; ((1 \leqslant i-1) \rightarrow (T(1) = 0) \; \& \ldots \& \; (T(i-1) = 0) \; \& \; (0 = 0))$$
$$\{T(i) := 0\} \; E(i/i+1),$$

whose precondition is equivalent to E.

This proves that condition E is an invariant of the loop. By applying the for loop rule, we then obtain:

$$(1 \leqslant \alpha \leqslant 0) \rightarrow (T(\alpha) = 0)$$
$$\{\textbf{for } i := 1 \textbf{ step } 1 \textbf{ to } n \textbf{ do } T(i) := 0\}$$
$$(1 > n) \; \& \; ((1 \leqslant \alpha \leqslant 0) \rightarrow (T(\alpha) = 0))$$
$$\vee \; (1 \leqslant n) \; \& \; ((1 \leqslant \alpha \leqslant n) \rightarrow (T(\alpha) = 0)).$$

Finally, this gives:

$$\text{true}$$
$$\{\textbf{for } i := 1 \textbf{ step } 1 \textbf{ to } n \textbf{ do } T(i) := 0\}$$
$$(n < 1) \vee ((T(1) = 0) \; \& \ldots \& \; (T(n) = 0))$$

Exercise

Deduce the preceding rule from the while loop rule (1.2.3.9).

3.3.4 Axioms for the instructions push and pop

The primitives *push* and *pop* have been described in section 2.3.1. The conditions concern the variables of the program, constants and particular variables: $p_1, p_2, p_3, \ldots$ and *tstack*.

The variable p_1 represents the top of the stack, p_2 the value below the top, etc. . . . The value of the variable *tstack* is the number of elements in the stack.

(1) One has *emptystack* $\sim$ (*tstack* $= 0$)

(2) One has the axiom E {*push*(*expr*)} S
where E is obtained from S by substituting
expr for p_1
p_{i-1} for p_i, for all $i > 1$
tstack+1 for *tstack*.
This can be denoted by:
$E \sim S(p_1/expr, p_2/p_1, p_3/p_2, \ldots \; tstack/tstack+1)$

(3) One has the axiom E {*pop*(x)}S
where E is obtained from S by substituting
p_1 for x
p_{i+1} for p_i, for all $i \geqslant 1$
tstack−1 for *tstack*.
This can be denoted by:
$E \sim S(x/p_1, p_1/p_2, p_2/p_3, \ldots \; tstack/tstack-1)$

Example
Take the sequence *push*(1); *push*(2); *pop*(x); *pop*(y) and the postcondition (x=2) & (y=1) & (*tstack*=0)

By using the above axioms and working through the sequence of substitutions, we obtain in succession the conditions:
(x=2) & (p_1=1) & (*tstack*−1=0), then (p_1=2) & (p_2=1) & (*tstack*−2=0), (2=2) & (p_1=1) & (*tstack*−1=0), and finally (2=2) & (1=1) & (*tstack*=0).
Hence:
(*tstack*=0) {*push*(1);*push*(2);*pop*(x);*pop*(y)} (x=2)&(y=1)&(*tstack*=0).

3.4. Proofs of programs containing procedure calls

3.4.1. Notations

We distinguish between formal variable parameters and formal value parameters. The first are synonyms of their actual parameters, which is to say that every reference (and in particular every assignment) to a formal variable parameter is in fact a reference (an assignment) to the corresponding actual parameter. The latter, on the contrary, denote variables local to the body of the procedure, which are given as initial values the values of their corresponding actual parameters. In particular, any assignment to a formal value parameter is an assignment to the local variable associated with this parameter, and does not modify the value of the corresponding actual parameter.

In what follows, actual variable parameters will be variables *without* indices, and actual value parameters expressions of any kind.

We shall consider a procedure defined in the following way:
procedure p (**variable** $x_1, x_2, \ldots, x_n$; **value** $y_1, y_2, \ldots, y_m$) ; Q, where
p is the name of the procedure,
$x_1, x_2, \ldots, x_n$, abbreviated as $\bar{x}$, is the list of variable parameters,
$y_1, y_2, \ldots, y_m$, written $\bar{y}$, is the list of value parameters,
Q is the body of the procedure.
A call of this procedure, $p(a_1, a_2, \ldots, a_n, e_1, e_2, \ldots, e_m)$ will be written $p(\bar{a},\bar{e})$, for short.

We shall also use the following example:

```
procedure div (integer value a, b ; integer variable q, r) ;
begin
  r := a ; q := 0 ;
 while r ≥ b do
     begin r := r−b ; q := q+1 end
end
```

3.4.2. Rules

The rules for procedure calls allow us to pass from a statement $E\{Q\}S$, proved for body Q of the procedure, to a statement of the form $E'\{p(\bar{a},\bar{e})\}\ S'$.

It would be simple to obtain E' and S' from E and S by substituting the actual parameters for the formal parameters. Unfortunately, this rule cannot be used in general: in the case of variable parameters, assignment axioms used in the proof of statement $E\{Q\}S$ may cease to make sense (see §3.2.3.5); in the case of value parameters, the actual parameters and the formal parameters are not synonyms.

Formal variable parameters
For a given call, the actual variable parameters are synonyms of the corresponding formal parameters. The following three conditions ensure that there are no other synonyms:

(i) No two actual variable parameters are synonyms.
(ii) No actual variable parameter is a synonym of a variable used in the body of the procedure.
(iii) No actual variable parameter is a synonym of a variable which appears in conditions E and S.

Condition (i) ensures that no two formal parameters are synonyms; conditions (ii) and (iii) ensure that no formal parameter is a synonym of a (non-local) variable appearing in Q, or in conditions E and S. These restrictions correspond to the normal use of procedures; for example, they exclude calls of the *div* procedure like $div(x, y, z, z)$.

Formal value parameters
The problem is that, in $E\{Q\}S$, S applies to the final values of the formal parameters, whereas in $E'\ \{p(\bar{a},\bar{e})\}\ S'$, S' applies to the final values of the actual parameters. Now, these values will be identical if the following two conditions are satisfied:

(iv) Formal value parameters are not modified by execution of Q.
(v) Actual value parameters which are expressions contain no operands which are actual variable parameters, or variables modified by execution of Q.

The following rule can be stated:

> If conditions (i) to (v) are satisfied, and if $E\{Q\}S$,
> then $E(\bar{x}/\bar{a},\ \bar{y}/\bar{e})\ \{p(\bar{a},\ \bar{e})\}\ S(\bar{x}/\bar{a},\ \bar{y}/\bar{e})$

where $E(\bar{x}/\bar{a},\ \bar{y}/\bar{e})$ and $S(\bar{x}/\bar{a},\ \bar{y}/\bar{e})$ are derived from E and S by replacing each occurrence of x_i by a_i, for $1 \leqslant i \leqslant n$, and each occurrence of y_i by e_i, for $1 \leqslant i \leqslant m$.

Example
If Q denotes the body of procedure *div*, we know (from Chapter 1) that:
$(a \geqslant 0)$ & $(b > 0)$ $\{Q\}$ $(a = bq + r)$ & $(0 \leqslant r < b)$.

The preceding rule immediately gives:
$(x+y \geqslant 0)$ & $(x-y > 0)$
$\{div(x+y, x-y, u, v)\}$
$(x+y = (x-y)u + v)$ & $(0 \leqslant v < x-y)$.

Remark
Even if conditions (i) to (v) are not all satisfied, it is possible that the proof of $E\{Q\}S$ will still be valid, and that the final values of the (actual and formal) value parameters will be identical. Having checked that this is so, the preceding rule may be applied.

When the value parameters satisfy condition (iv), but not condition (v), the following rule should be used:

If conditions (i) to (iv) are satisfied, and if $E\{Q\}S$, then $E(\bar{x}/\bar{a}, \bar{y}/\bar{e})$ & $(\bar{u} = \bar{u}_0)$ $\{p(\bar{a},\bar{e})\}$ $S(\bar{x}/\bar{a}, \bar{y}/\bar{e}')$

where
$\bar{u}$ is the set of variables which appear in expressions of $\bar{e}$,
$\bar{u}_0$ is a set of variables which does not appear in Q, $\bar{a}$, $\bar{e}$, E, S,
$\bar{e}'$ is the list of expressions $\bar{e}'_i$, $1 \leqslant i \leqslant m$,
where e'_i is derived from e_i by replacing each occurrence of a variable of $\bar{u}$ by the corresponding variable of $\bar{u}_0$.

Example
For the call $div(x+y, x, x, v)$, we obtain:
$(x+y \geqslant 0)$ & $(x > 0)$ & $(x = x_0)$ & $(y = y_0)$
$\{div(x+y, x, x, v)\}$
$(x_0+y_0 = x_0x + v)$ & $(0 \leqslant v < x_0)$.

Remarks
(1) The two rules can obviously be combined if the value parameters do not all satisfy condition (v). So, for the call $div(x, y, x, t)$, we get:
$(x \geqslant 0)$ & $(y > 0)$ & $(x = x_0)$
$\{div(x, y, x, t)\}$
$(x_0 = yx + t)$ & $(0 \leqslant t < y)$.
(2) If condition S contains no occurrence of a formal value parameter, there is no point in introducing the condition $(\bar{u} = \bar{u}_0)$ and the previous rule can be used.

Thus, from
$(a \geqslant 0)$ & $(b > 0)$ $\{Q\}$ $(q \geqslant 0)$ & $(r \geqslant 0)$
we deduce
$(x+y \geqslant 0)$ & $(x > 0)$ $\{div(x+y, x, x, v)\}$ $(x \geqslant 0)$ & $(v \geqslant 0)$.

Exercises

(1) What conditions must the parameters satisfy for the following rule to be valid?

If E $\{Q\}$ S then $E(\bar{x}/\bar{a},\ \bar{y}/\bar{e})$ $\{p(\bar{a},\ \bar{e})\}$ $(\exists \bar{u}_1,\ S(\bar{x}/\bar{a},\ \bar{y}/\bar{e}''))$

where

$\bar{u}_1$ is a set of variables which does not appear in Q, $\bar{a}$, $\bar{e}$, E, S,
$\bar{e}''$ is the list of expressions e''_i, $1 \leqslant i \leqslant m$, where e''_i is derived from e_i by replacing each occurrence of a variable of $\bar{u}$ by the corresponding variable of $\bar{u}_1$ ($\bar{u}$ is the set of variables which appear in the expressions of $\bar{e}$).

(2) Take the following procedure definition:

procedure p (**integer variable** r ; **integer value** x, y) ;
  begin $x := y+1$; $r := x$ **end**

Prove the following statements:

$(a = a_0)$ $\{p(r,\ a,\ a)\}$ $(r = a_0 + 1)$
$(a > 0)$ $\{p(r,\ a,\ a)\}$ $(r > 0)$.

3.4.3. Proofs of termination

Consider a procedure p. A call of p may not terminate if the body Q of the procedure involves a loop, **while** B **do** R. To prove the termination of a loop (section 1.3), we made use of the existence of an invariant condition for that loop. In the same way, to prove the termination of Q, we shall determine a condition E (depending on the program variables and formal parameters of p) invariant for the loop. We shall define a mapping v from $(W \times X)_{E\&B}$ to $\mathbb{N}$ such that

$$E \ \&\ B \ \&\ (v(w) = v_0)\ \{R\}\ \neg B \vee (v(w) < v_0),$$

where $(W \times X)_{E\&B}$ is the set of values of the program variables and parameters of p satisfying the condition $E\&B$.

Termination is then proved if condition E is true before execution of the loop. This allows us to determine a precondition F of Q which ensures termination. Condition F applies to the variables of the program and the formal parameters of p.

For a given call of p, we substitute the actual parameters for the formal parameters in F. If the condition obtained (which depends only on the program variables) is satisfied at the time of the call, then the latter terminates.

Remark

In the case of synonymy, the proof may be incorrect. To avoid the possibility, we make sure that the call respects constraints (i) and (ii) of Section 3.4.2.

Example

To prove the termination of the body of procedure *div* (see Section 1.3.2), we can use the loop invariant $(b > 0)$ and the function $v(w) = r$. Then, to ensure termination, we simply have to take condition $(b > 0)$ as a precondition of Q.

The call $div(x, y, u, w)$ therefore terminates if condition $(y > 0)$ is satisfied at the point of call, and $div(x+y, x-y, x, y)$ terminates if $(x > y)$.

3.5. Analysis of programs involving procedure calls

3.5.1. Analysis of execution time

The execution time of a procedure call can be defined as the sum of the execution time of the body of the procedure and the time needed for parameter passing. The execution time of the body of a procedure is defined as the execution time of an iterative program, the parameters being considered as variables.

3.5.2. Analysis of storage space

We shall only discuss the case of procedures which do not contain instructions for the allocation or deallocation of storage, other than declarations of variables at the head of the block.

The space needed to execute a procedure call can be defined as the space needed to execute the body of the procedure, plus a constant amount of space (to contain, for example, the values of the value parameters, the addresses of the variable parameters and the return address after execution of the body of the procedure).

The space required to execute body Q of a procedure, the values of the program variables and value parameters at the moment of the call (w) is given by:

$$N_Q(w) = d_0(w) + \text{Max}\,(N_{b_1}(f_1(w)), \ldots, N_{b_n}(f_n(w)), N_{a_1}(f_{n+1}(w)), \ldots, N_{a_k}(f_{n+k}(w)))$$

where:

d_0 is the space occupied by the variables declared in Q (if Q is not a block, $d_0 = 0$),

$b_1, \ldots, b_n$, $(n \geqslant 0)$, are the n blocks of Q, not embedded and executed in succession, for w,

$a_1, \ldots, a_k$, $(k \geqslant 0)$, are the k procedure calls, contained in the body Q, but not in a block embedded in Q, executed for w,

$f_1(w), \ldots, f_{n+k}(w)$ are the values of the program variables and the value parameters of the procedure, computed respectively on activation of blocks $b_1, \ldots, b_n$ and at the calls $a_1, \ldots, a_k$.

Commentary and Bibliography

There have been numerous studies of Hoare's method. For an overall view, see Apt's article (Apt, 1981).

A method for proving total correctness using weakest preconditions is described in Dijkstra's book (Dijkstra, 1976).

Among other methods for proving programs, one can mention the method of intermittent assertions defined by Burstall (1974) and developed by Manna and Waldinger (1978), and the method of structural induction (Burstall, 1969). The latter is used in this book for proofs of termination.

These methods do not deal with properties other than partial or total correctness of programs. There are more general logical systems which allow us to deal with other properties such as the equivalence of programs: for example, algorithmic logic (Banachowski *et al.*, 1977) and dynamic logic (Harel, 1979). For an overall view of program proofs, see the article by Harel (1980) and the books by Manna (1974) and Livercy (1978). For further material on the analysis of programs, consult the books by Knuth (1969; 1973), by Aho *et al.* (1974; 1983), and the article by Tarjan (1978).

Chapter 4

Proof and Analysis of Recursive Programs

4.1. Introduction

4.1.1.

A *recursive program* is a program which contains one or more recursive procedures. A procedure p is said to be *recursive* if its execution can invoke one or more calls of p. These calls are said to be *recursive calls*. On the other hand, a procedure call, occurring when the procedure is not already being executed, will be termed a *principal call*. We distinguish between

simple recursions, where all the recursive calls appear in the body of the same procedure, and
simultaneous recursions, where recursive calls are invoked by the execution of other procedures called in the body of the recursive procedure. For example, the body of a procedure p contains a call to a procedure q, which in turn contains a call to procedure p.

In this chapter, we shall consider only simple recursions, being those most commonly found in practice. Simultaneous recursions do not really present any further difficulties.

Example of a recursive procedure
Procedure m below contains two recursive calls. It calculates the product of two non-negative integers in a similar way to program $M5$ in section 2.4.1.

```
procedure m (integer value x, y ; integer variable r) ;
if y = 0 then r := 0
else if even(y) then m (x * 2,y div 2,r)
    else begin m(x * 2, y div 2, r) ; r := r+x end
```

4.1.2. Execution trees of a recursive procedure

It is sometimes convenient to represent the sequence of recursive calls and instructions executed via a call to a recursive procedure by a tree, constructed as follows:

> The call in question is the label for the root of the tree.
> The leaves of the tree are labelled with sequences of instructions, and the other vertices by procedure calls.
> If the call in question does not invoke a recursive call, then the root leads only to a leaf, which is labelled with the associated sequence of instructions.

On the other hand, if at least one recursive call is invoked, the root will lead to the following (from left to right):

> a leaf labelled with the sequence of instructions executed before the first recursive call;
> a vertex labelled with the first recursive call, linked to an appropriate subtree of calls;
> a leaf labelled with the sequence of instructions executed after the first recursive procedure, and before the following call;
> a vertex labelled with the following recursive call, and connecting with the tree of corresponding calls;
> . . .
> a leaf labelled with the sequence of instructions executed when all the recursive calls invoked by the call in question have ended.

Note: If one of the sequences of instructions being considered is empty, the corresponding leaf will not appear in the tree.

Example
For the call $m(5, 5, res)$ of the above procedure, we obtain the following execution tree:

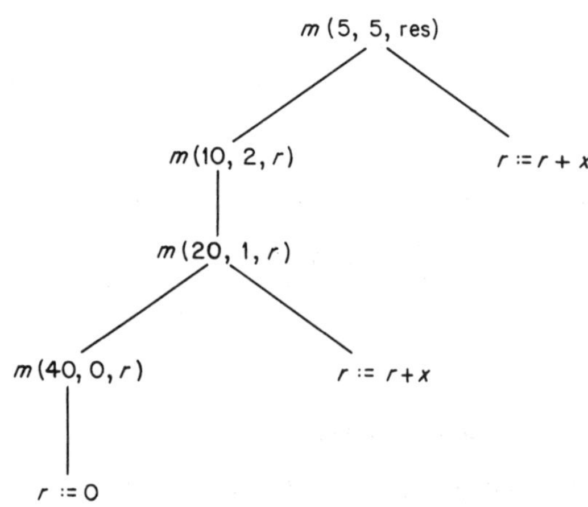

Remarks

An execution tree can be infinite, in which the case the corresponding call loops.

It is not always possible to construct an execution tree: for instance, if the values of certain tests, which are needed to determine the actual recursive calls ($y=0$ and even(y) for procedure m), depend on the inputs of the program.

It follows that, for each principal call, we will often be interested in the collection of possible execution trees.

In the case of m, this collection can be described informally, for all integers a, b, and res, by:

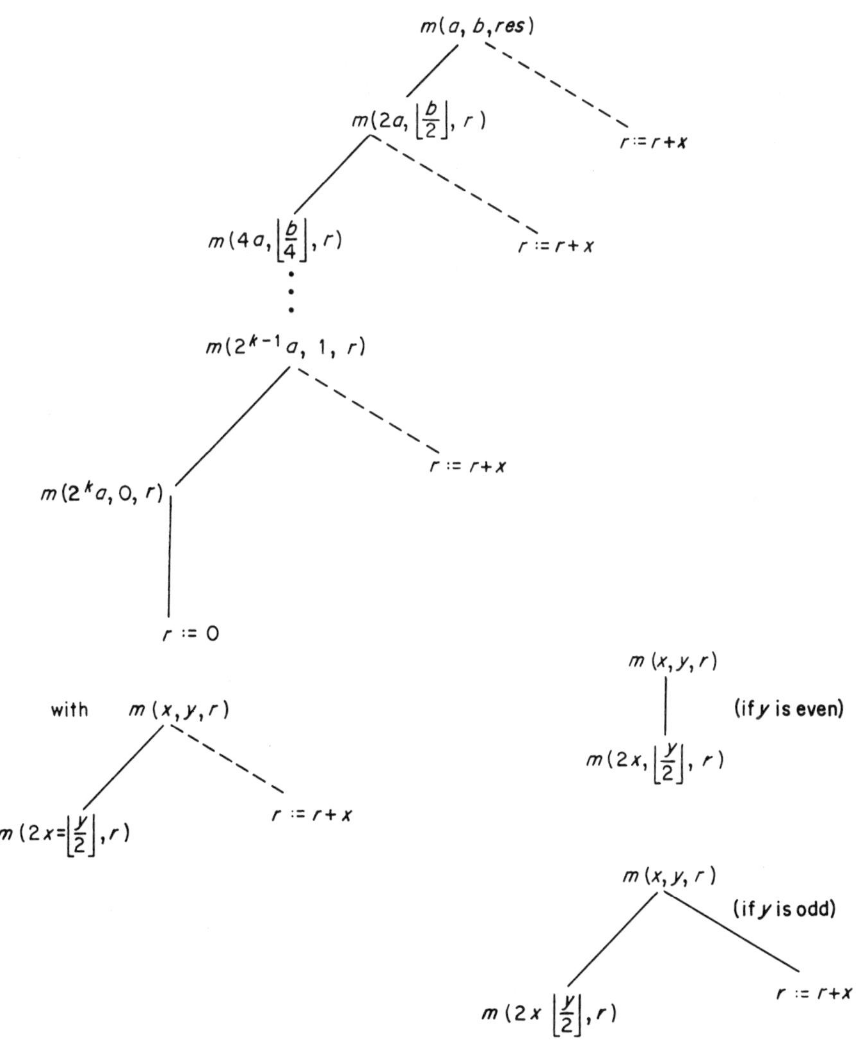

It is difficult, except in simple cases, to characterize the collection of execution trees for a recursive program. We shall see in the following sections that in order to prove, analyse, or construct a recursive program, it is better to argue recursively on the body of the procedure than to 'set out' the recursions, as we do when constructing the execution tree.

4.1.3. Computation of a recursive procedure for a principal call

Consider

- a recursive procedure where the tests do not modify the values of the variables and parameters,
- a principal call of this procedure, and
- the execution tree for this principal call.

The computation sequence of the procedure for the principal call can be determined in the following way:

(a) Traverse all the paths of the tree, beginning at the root. Replace, in each successor of a vertex corresponding to a call,
  - the variable parameters by the corresponding actual parameters;
  - the value parameters, and the variables declared in the body of the procedure, by variables not yet used.

    Initializations of variables associated with value parameters should be added.

(b) Execute the leaves of this transformed execution tree from left to right.

Example
The execution tree of example 4.1.2 is shown below.

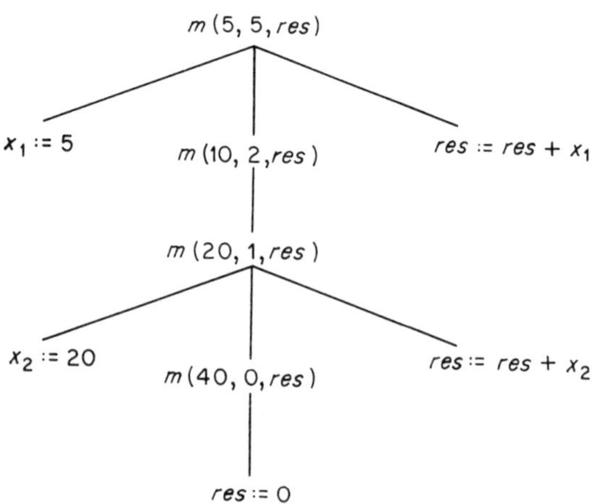

(Note: For simplicity's sake, we have not initialized variables which do not appear in the leaves.)

The following sequence of instructions is obtained:

$x_1 := 5$; $x_2 := 20$; $res := 0$; $res := res + x_2$; $res := res + x_1$

After execution, we have: $res = 25 = 5 \times 5$.

4.1.4. Call trees of a recursive procedure

We are often not interested in the vertices of the execution tree labelled with sequences of instructions (which do not contain a recursive call). The name *call tree* is given to a tree obtained from the execution tree, retaining only the vertices labelled with procedure calls.

Example

For the call $m(5, 5, res)$, we obtain the following tree:

$$
\begin{array}{c}
m(5, 5, res) \\
| \\
m(10, 2, r) \\
| \\
m(20, 1, r) \\
| \\
m(40, 0, r)
\end{array}
$$

4.1.5. Depth of a recursive call—Embedded recursive calls

The depth of a recursive call is the length of the path which connects the root to the vertex associated with the call in the call tree. A principal call is therefore always at depth 0. In the above example, the call $m(40, 0, r)$ is at depth 3.

Two calls are embedded if one is invoked by the execution of the other, or equivalently, if there is a path linking them in the call tree. In the above example, all calls are embedded.

4.2. Proofs of partial correctness of recursive procedures

In section 3.4.2, we looked at rules for proving the correctness of a procedure call, the body of the procedure having been proved correct. These rules also apply in the case of recursive procedures, with the same restrictions on the use of parameters. But we need a new rule for proving the body of the procedure, because of the recursive calls which this contains.

Suppose we have proved the body of a recursive procedure p, under the hypothesis that all the recursive calls are themselves correct. What can we then conclude about any one call p_0 of this procedure?

Let T_0 be the execution tree associated with p_0.

(a) If T_0 is of the form:

where α contains no recursive call, then α has been proved, and it follows that p_0 is correct.
(b) If T_0 is of the form:

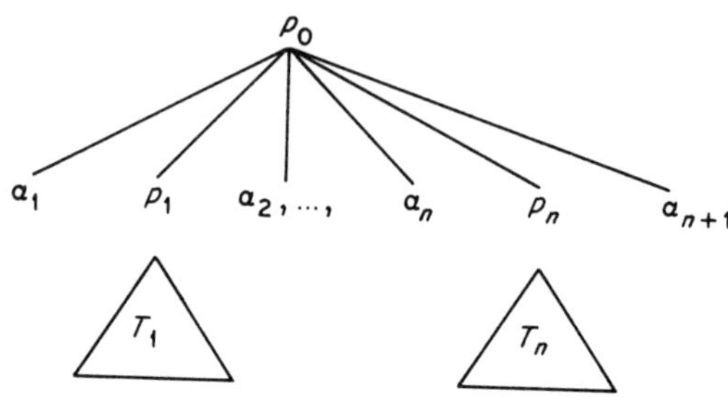

where $p_1, p_2, \ldots, p_n$ are calls of p, and where $\alpha_1, \alpha_2, \ldots, \alpha_{n+1}$ contain no recursive calls, then the sequence $\alpha_1\ p_1\ \alpha_2, \ldots, p_n\ \alpha_{n+1}$ has been proved correct, under the hypothesis that $p_1, p_2, \ldots, p_n$ were correct. Therefore, p_0 is correct if $p_1, p_2, \ldots, p_n$ are correct, and so our obligation is to prove the calls $p_1, p_2, \ldots, p_n$. Consider the trees $T_1, T_2, \ldots, T_n$, in the same way as we have done for T_0. Now, assuming T_0 is finite (we are carrying out a proof of partial correctness), the trees $T_1, T_2, \ldots, T_n$ contain strictly fewer vertices than T_0. Reasoning inductively on the number of vertices of T_0, and using (a), we can therefore conclude that p_0 is correct.

Informally, we therefore have the following rule:

If, under the hypothesis that all the recursive calls are correct, one can prove that the body of the procedure is correct, then the body of the procedure is correct.

To state this rule more formally, we make use of the notations of sections 3.4.1 and 3.4.2.

Let (h) be the condition:

> for every call $p(\bar{a}, \bar{e})$ satisfying conditions (i) to (v) of section 3.4.2, one has $E(\bar{x}/\bar{a}, \bar{y}/\bar{e})\ \{p(\bar{a}, \bar{e})\}\ S(\bar{x}/\bar{a}, \bar{y}/\bar{e})$.

We then have the following rule:

If, under hypothesis (h), one can prove $E\{Q\}S$, then one has $E\{Q\}S$.

Condition (h) is called the induction hypothesis.

For recursive calls which do not satisfy conditions (i) to (v), we shall attempt to adapt hypothesis (h) (see remarks made in section 3.4.2).

4.3. Example

We are going to carry out the proof of partial correctness of procedure m, defined in section 4.1.1. We have to prove that:

$(x \geq 0)$ & $(y \geq 0)$ $\{Q\}$ $(r = xy)$, where Q is the body of procedure m. According to the conditional rule, it is sufficient to prove:

(a) $(x \geq 0)$ & $(y \geq 0)$ & $(y=0)$
$\{r := 0\}$
$(r = xy)$

(b) $(x \geq 0)$ & $(y \geq 0)$ & $(y \neq 0)$ & $even(y)$
$\{m(x*2,\ y$ **div** $2,\ r)\}$
$(r = xy)$

(c) $(x \geq 0)$ & $(y \geq 0)$ & $(y \neq 0)$ & $\neg\, even(y)$
$\{m(x*2,\ y$ **div** $2,\ r)\ ;\ r := r+x\}$
$(r = xy)$

Conditions (i), (iv), and (v) are satisfied by the two recursive calls, but conditions (ii) and (iii) are not. However, the formal parameter r is not a synonym of any other variable. The induction hypothesis (h) can therefore be used to prove (b) and (c).

(a) We have: $(0 = xy)$ $\{r := 0\}$ $(r = xy)$
and $(x \geq 0)$ & $(y \geq 0)$ & $(y = 0) \rightarrow (0 = xy)$.

(b) According to the induction hypothesis, the recursive call $m(x*2,\ y$ **div** $2,\ r)$ is correct, that is to say:
$(2x \geq 0)$ & $(\lfloor y/2 \rfloor \geq 0)$ $\{m(x*2,\ y$ **div** $2,\ r)\}$ $(r = 2x.\lfloor y/2 \rfloor)$
On the other hand,
$even(y)$
$\{m(x*2,\ y$ **div** $2,\ r)\}$
$even(y)$,
since $m(x*2,\ y$ **div** $2,\ r)$ satisfies condition (v) of paragraph 3.4.2.
So:
$(2x \geq 0)$ & $(\lfloor y/2 \rfloor \geq 0)$ & $even(y)$
$\{m(x*2,\ y$ **div** $2,\ r)\}$
$(r=2x.\lfloor y/2 \rfloor)$ & $even(y)$
Now $(x \geq 0)$ & $(y \geq 0) \sim (2x \geq 0)$ & $(\lfloor y/2 \rfloor \geq 0)$
and $((r = 2x.\lfloor y/2 \rfloor)$ & $even(y)) \rightarrow (r = 2x.y/2) \sim (r = xy)$

(c) According to the induction hypothesis, and since
$m(x*2,\ y$ **div** $2,\ r)$ satisfies (v) 3.4.2, we deduce:
$(2x \geq 0)$ & $(\lfloor y/2 \rfloor) \geq 0)$ & $\neg\, even(y)$
$\{m(x*2,\ y$ **div** $2,\ r)\}$
$(r = 2x.\lfloor y/2 \rfloor)$ & $\neg\, even(y)$

Now, $(x \geqslant 0)$ & $(y \geqslant 0) \sim (2x \geqslant 0)$ & $(\lfloor y/2 \rfloor \geqslant 0)$
and furthermore,
$(r=(2x.\lfloor y/2 \rfloor)$ & $\neg\, even(y)) \rightarrow (\exists t, (r=2tx)$ & $(y = 2t+1))$
Hence:
$(x \geqslant 0)$ & $(y \geqslant 0)$ & $(y \neq 0)$ & $\neg\, even(y)$
$\{m(x{*}2, y$ **div** $2, r)\}$
$(\exists t, (r=2tx)$ & $(y=2t+1))$
On the other hand,
$(r+x = xy)\ \{r := r+x)\ (r = xy)$
and
$(\exists t, (r = 2tx)$ & $(y = 2t+1)$
$\quad \rightarrow (\exists t, (r+x = 2tx + x)$ & $(y = 2t+1))$
$\quad \rightarrow (\exists t, (r+x = x(2t+1))$ & $(y = 2t+1))$
$\quad \rightarrow (r+x = xy)$.

4.4. Proof of termination of a recursive procedure

We shall only deal with the case of recursive procedures which contain no **goto** instructions or tests which modify the values of the variables of the program (or parameters).

4.4.1. Proof of termination of a recursive procedure without loops

Let p be such a procedure. A principal call of p can give an infinite sequence of calculations only if it invokes an infinite sequence of embedded calls.

Consider a condition E (containing the program variables and formal parameters of p), such that if E is true before execution of the body of procedure p, then for every recursive call $p(\bar{a}, \bar{e})$, condition $E(\bar{x}/\bar{a}, \bar{y}/\bar{e})$ is true after the execution of this call.

This condition plays the same role as the loop invariant used in section 3.4.3.

Let p_0 be a call of p, and $w_0 \in (W \times X)_E$ the values of the variables at the point of call of p_0, and of the parameters of p_0. We shall denote the recursive calls of p which are the 'sons' of p_0 in the call tree by $p_1, p_2, \ldots, p_k$, $(k \geqslant 0)$, and the values of the variables and parameters at point of call by $w_1, w_2, \ldots, w_k$. Clearly, $w_1, w_2, \ldots, w_k \in (W \times X)_E$.

Suppose now that there exists a function v from $(W \times X)_E$ to $\mathbb{N}$, with the following property:

for every $w_0 \in (W \times X)_E$, we have
$\quad v(w_0) > v(w_1), v(w_0) > v(w_2), \ldots, v(w_0) > v(w_k)$.
In this case a (recursive or principal) call $p(\bar{a}, \bar{e})$ terminates if condition $E(\bar{x}/\bar{a}, \bar{y}/\bar{e})$ is satisfied before execution.

Indeed, the value of function v is strictly decreasing whenever we pass from a call of p to an embedded recursive call, and under these conditions it is clear that there cannot exist an infinite path in the call tree.

Example
Consider a program containing three variables a, b and res of type **integer**, and a call $m(a, b, res)$, where procedure m is defined in section 4.1.1.

If condition $E = (x \geqslant 0) \mathbin{\&} (y \geqslant 0)$ is true before execution of the body of m, then the condition $(2x \geqslant 0) \mathbin{\&} (\lfloor y/w \rfloor \geqslant 0)$ is true before all recursive calls.

We have $(W \times X)_E = Z \times Z \times Z \times \mathbb{N} \times \mathbb{N} \times Z$.
We can use function $v : (W \times X)_E \to \mathbb{N}$, defined by

$$v(a, b, res, x, y, r) = y.$$

The call $m(a, b, res)$ therefore terminates if precondition $(a \geqslant 0) \mathbin{\&} (b \geqslant 0)$ is satisfied.

4.4.2. Proof of termination of a recursive procedure with loops

Let p be such a recursive procedure. A principal call of p can give rise to an infinite sequence of computations only if

(a) it gives rise to an infinite sequence of embedded recursive calls, or if
(b) the body of a while loop, in the principal call or one of the recursive calls, is executed an infinite number of times.

To prove that case (a) cannot arise, we proceed as in section 4.4.1. For case (b), we adapt the method given in section 3.4.3 to prove the termination of a non-recursive procedure.

Condition F, which is then defined to ensure termination of the loop, must be such that: if F is true before execution of the body of p, then condition $F(\bar{x}/\bar{a}, \bar{y}/\bar{e})$ is true before execution of all recursive calls $p(\bar{a}, \bar{e})$. In this way, the termination of the loop is also proved for all the embedded recursive calls.

Remark
If there are synonyms, the proof may not be correct. This can be avoided by making all calls obey constraints (i) and (ii) of section 3.4.2.

4.5. Analysis of a recursive procedure

4.5.1. Analysis of execution time

The execution time of a procedure call was defined in section 3.5.1. In the case of a call of a recursive procedure, this definition does not yield the execution time directly, but *a recurrence relation which gives the execution time as its solution.*

Example
If we denote the body of procedure m as described in section 4.1.1 by Q, the execution time of any call $m(u, v, t)$ will be given by $T_{m(u,v,t)}\ (w) = T_Q\ (w,x,y,r) + T_{x,y,r/u,v,t}$ where

- w represents the values of the program variables before the call $m(u, v, t)$,
- $T_Q\ (w, x, y, r)$ the execution time of the body of m,
- $T_{x, y, r/u, v, t}$ the time for passing parameters.

Execution time $T_{Q\ (w,x,y,r)}$ is the solution to the following recurrence relation:

if $y = 0$, $\quad T_Q\ (w,x,y,r) = T_{y=0} + T_{r:=0}$

if $y = 2n,\ n \geqslant 1$, $\quad T_Q\ (w,x,y,r) = T_{y=0} + T_{even} + T_{m(x*2,y\ \mathbf{div}\ 2,r)}\ (w)$

if $y = 2n+1,\ n \geqslant 0$, $\quad T_Q\ (w,x,y,r) = T_{y=0} + T_{even} + T_{r:=r+x} + T_{m(x*2,y\ \mathbf{div}\ 2,r)}\ (w)$

This relation can be put in the form:

$T_Q(y) = K_1,$ if $y = 0$,

$\quad = T_Q(n) + K_2,$ if $y = 2n,\ n \geqslant 1$,

$\quad = T_Q(n) + K_3,$ if $y = 2n+1,\ n \geqslant 0$.

It is easy to deduce that $T_Q\ (w,x,y,r)$ is of order (log y).

4.5.2. Analysis of storage space

The space needed to execute a procedure call was defined in section 3.5.2. In the case of a call of a recursive procedure, the memory requirements cannot be obtained directly: again we obtain a recurrence relation which gives this value as its solution.

Example

Consider the call $m(u, v, t)$ of the procedure defined in section 4.1, w being the values of the program variables at the point of call. We have:

$$N_{m(u,v,t)}\ (w) = N_Q\ (w, x, y, r) + 4,$$

assuming that four store locations are needed for the parameters and the return address.

$N_Q(w,x,y,r) = 0,$ if $(y = 0)$,

$\quad = N_{m(x*2,\ y\ \mathbf{div}\ 2,r)}\ (w)$ if $(y \neq 0)$.

From this we deduce:

$N_{m(u,v,t)}\ (w) = 4,$ if $v = 0$,

$\quad = 4 + N_{m(u*2,v\ \mathbf{div}\ 2,r)}\ (w),$ if $v \neq 0$.

The result is that the space required to execute $m(u,v,t)$ is of order (log v).

Comments and Bibliography

The rule for proving the partial correctness of recursive procedures is due to Hoare (1971). It is an application of Scott's induction rule (Livercy, 1978). It is insufficient for proving formally properties relating to the values of global variables before and after executing a call of a recursive procedure (for more details, consult the article by Apt (1981). Such properties will be used in the last chapter (§ 6.3.1.5), and will be proved with the help of an informal argument based on the rule given here.

The method for proving termination is based on the same principle as that used to prove the termination of iterative programs: it is justified by induction over the set of program inputs, and can be formalized (see Apt, 1981).

For the solution of recurrence relations, the reader can consult the books by Liu (1977), Greene and Knuth (1981), and Aho *et al.* (1974; 1983). Sample solutions are given in Chapter 5.

Chapter 5

Construction of Recursive Programs

5.1. Principles of construction

As in the case of iterative programs (see Chapter 2), it is more efficient to construct a recursive program and its proof at the same time than to prove *a posteriori* a program which has already been written.

For the solution of a problem P, the construction of a recursive procedure and its proof is based

(a) on the direct solution of P in certain particular cases, and

(b) on the choice of a decomposition of P into sub-problems of the same kind as P, such that successive decompositions always lead to one of the cases referred to in (a).

The procedure then contains:

- Instructions which directly solve the particular cases (a).
- Instructions which decompose the problem into sub-problems, and solve it from the solutions to these sub-problems (b).
- Recursive calls which solve these sub-problems.

For example, procedure m of section 4.1 solves the problem of computing the product of two integers x and y, directly if $y = 0$, and by solving the sub-problem 'compute the product of $2x$ and $\lfloor y/2 \rfloor$' otherwise.

A proof of partial correctness consists in showing that the chosen decomposition, when it converges, does in fact solve problem P. Proof of termination consists in verifying that the chosen decomposition converges, that is to say successive decomposition (b) always leads to one of the particular cases (a). This means the recursive sub-problems must be somehow 'closer' to the directly solvable cases than the initial problem. This can be formalized by attributing to the initial problem a 'size', measured by a strictly positive integer n, such that all sub-problems have sizes strictly smaller than n. By convention, we suppose the directly solvable problems have size 1.

For example, in procedure m, the size of the problem 'calculate the product of x and y' can be taken to be $y + 1$.

In general, one can choose from a large number of possible ways of decomposing a problem into sub-problems. In the following section, we give a few rules for choosing efficient decompositions. For each decomposition, we shall analyse the execution time as a function of the size of the problem. For these analyses to be comparable, the size must be defined independently of the decomposition. For instance, it is usual to define the size of a sorting problem by the number of elements to be sorted.

5.1.1. First case. 'Logarithmic reduction'

Suppose that, to solve a given problem of size n, we can choose between the following two decompositions:

(i) If $n > 1$, solve the same problem of size $n-1$, and then process it in a time given by a function $f(n)$;
if $n = 1$, solve the problem directly in time c.

The execution time of the recursive procedure written according to this decomposition will be the solution to the equation:

$$T(n) = T(n-1) + f(n)$$
$$T(1) = c$$

The solution to this equation is $T(n) = c + \sum_{i=2}^{n} f(i)$.

(ii) (Suppose, to simplify matters, that $n = 2^k$.)
If $n > 1$, solve the same problem of size $n/2$, and then process it in a time given by a function $g(n)$;
if $n = 1$, solve the problem (as in case (i)) in time c.

The execution time of the recursive procedure written according to this decomposition will be the solution to the equation:

$$T(n) = T\left(\frac{n}{2}\right) + g(n)$$

$$T(1) = c$$

As $n = 2^k$, the solution is

$$T(n) = c + \sum_{i=1}^{k} g(2^i)$$

Solution (ii) is therefore preferable to solution (i), whenever functions f and g are of the same order.

For example, if functions $f(n)$ and $g(n)$ are constants, $T(n)$ is order n in case (i), but order ($\log n$) in case (ii).

Choosing decomposition (ii) rather than decomposition (i) therefore amounts to carrying out a logarithmic reduction of a program written according to decomposition (i). We should note, however, a difference of approach: in the one case, we construct a 'good' program directly, whereas in the other case, we first construct a 'bad' program, which is then transformed into a 'good' one.

When n is not a power of 2, we can usually apply decomposition (ii) by reducing it to a sub-problem whose size is as close as possible to $n/2$; the execution time is then of the same order as if $n = 2^k$ (see the logarithmic reductions of Chapter 2 and the binary program in section 5.3).

5.1.2. Second case

Now suppose that, to solve a problem of size n, we have the choice between:
(i) Decomposition (i) of section 5.1.1, with $f(n) = n$.

The execution time is then the solution to the equation:

$$T(n) = T(n-1) + n$$
$$T(1) = c$$

which is $T(n) = c + 2 + 3 + \ldots + n$, i.e. order n^2.

(ii) The following decomposition (we suppose $n = 2^k$): if $n > 1$, solve the two sub-problems of size $n/2$ and then process them in time order n; if $n = 1$, solve directly in time c.

The execution time is then the solution to the equation:

$$T(n) = 2T\left(\frac{n}{2}\right) + n$$

$$T(1) = c$$

The solution can be determined as follows:

$$T(2^k) = 2.T(2^{k-1}) + 2^k$$
$$2.T(2^{k-1}) = 2^2.T(2^{k-2}) + 2.2^{k-1}$$
$$\cdots\cdots$$
$$2^iT(2^{k-i}) = 2^{i+1}.T(2^{k-(i+1)}) + 2^i.2^{k-i}$$
$$\cdots\cdots$$
$$2^{k-1}.T(2^{k-(k-1)}) = 2^k.T(1) + 2^{k-1}.2k(k-1)$$
$$2^k.T(1) = 2^k.c$$

Hence $T(2^k) = 2^k . c + k.2^k$

$T(n)$ is therefore order ($n \log n$), and so, decomposition (ii) is preferable to decomposition (i), for sufficiently large n.

An example of a program based on decomposition (i) would be sorting by insertion; and one based on decomposition (ii) would be sorting by merging. (See also section 5.4 on sorting by partitioning.)

5.1.3. Generalization

We saw in 5.1.2 that it is preferable to decompose a problem of size n into two sub-problems of equal size (scheme (ii)) rather than into one sub-problem of size $n-1$ and another of size 1 (which corresponds to scheme (i)). This is an instance of a general principle, several applications of which will be given in this chapter: a recursive decomposition of a problem into sub-problems of equal size leads to efficient algorithms. The decomposition consists in dividing a problem of size n ($n > 1$) into sub-problems of size n/b (on the assumption that n is a power of b). Assuming the division of a problem of size n, together with its solution from the solution of the sub-problems, takes time $f(n)$, the execution time of the associated recursive procedure is given by the equation:

$$T(n) = a\,T\left(\frac{n}{b}\right) + f(n)$$
$$T(1) = c$$

The following lemma gives the solutions to this equation in the case where $f(n)$ is order n.

Lemma

The equation $\quad T(n) = a\,T\left(\frac{n}{b}\right) + n$ (with $a > 1$ and $b > 1$)
$\quad T(1) = c$

has a solution
- of order n, if $a < b$
- of order $(n \log n)$, if $a = b$
- of order $(n^{\log_b a})$, if $a > b$

Proof

(In what follows, $\log_b x$ will be written simply as $\log x$.)
Supposing n is a power of b, we have:

$$T(n) = a\,T\left(\frac{n}{b}\right) + n$$

$$a\,T\left(\frac{n}{b}\right) = a^2 T\left(\frac{n}{b^2}\right) + a$$

$$\cdots\cdots$$

$$a^i T\left(\frac{n}{b^i}\right) = a^{i+1}\,T\left(\frac{n}{b^{i+1}}\right) + \frac{a^i}{b^i}\,n$$

$$\cdots\cdots$$

$$a^{\log(n-1)}\,T\left(\frac{n}{b^{\log(n-1)}}\right) = a^{\log n}\,T\left(\frac{n}{b^{\log n}}\right) + \frac{a^{\log(n-1)}}{b^{\log(n-1)}}\,.\,n$$

$$a^{\log n}\,T(1) = a^{\log n}.c$$

Hence

$$T(n) = n \sum_{i=0}^{\log(n-1)} \left(\frac{a}{b}\right)^i + a^{\log n}.c$$

if $a < b$, then $a^{\log n} < n$,

and, as the series $\sum_{i=0}^{\infty} \left(\frac{a}{b}\right)^i$ converges,

$T(n)$ is of order n.

if $a = b$, then $T(n) = n \sum_{i=0}^{\log(n-1)} 1 + n.c$

$T(n)$ is therefore of order $(n \log n)$.
if $a > b$, then

$$\sum_{i=0}^{\log(n-1)} \left(\frac{a}{b}\right)^i = \frac{\left(\frac{a}{b}\right)^{\log n} - 1}{\frac{a}{b} - 1} \text{ is of order } \left(\frac{a}{b}\right)^{\log n} = \frac{a^{\log n}}{n}$$

It follows that $n \sum_{i=0}^{\log(n-1)} \left(\frac{a}{b}\right)^i$ is of order $(a^{\log_b n})$,

and therefore $T(n)$ is of order $(a^{\log_b n})$, or equivalently, $(n^{\log_b n})$.

5.1.4. 'Dynamic programming'

In our discussion of a recursive decomposition for a given problem, we have so far only taken into account (i) the size of the problems to be solved and (ii) the time required for the decomposition of the initial problem, and its solution from the solutions to the sub-problems. This is not always enough: some decompositions can lead to inefficient programs because they solve the same sub-problem more than once.

Example
Consider a recursive program for calculating the number of combinations of p objects chosen from among n, based on the following recurrence relation:

(i) for $0 < p < n$, $C_n^p = C_{n-1}^p + C_{n-1}^{p-1}$
(ii) for $p = 0$ or $p = n$, $C_n^p = 1$

Such a program will certainly not be optimal in execution time. Indeed, a call tree will take the form shown below.

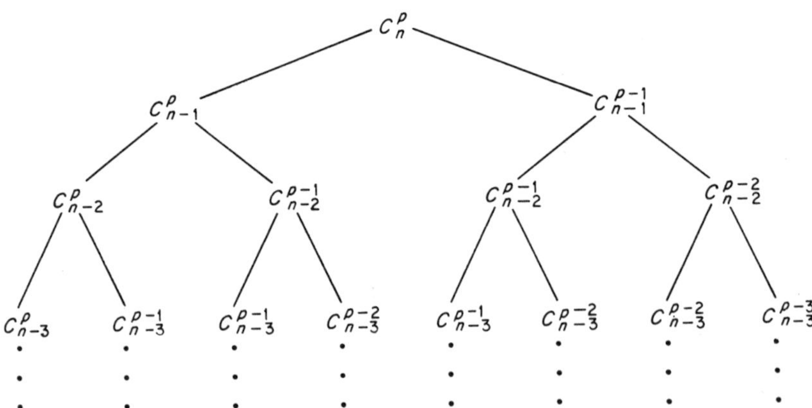

The values of C^{p-1}_{n-2}, C^{p-1}_{n-3}, C^{p-2}_{n-3}, ... are therefore calculated more than once.

In sections 5.5 and 5.6 we give examples of non-optimal recursive programs and equivalent optimized recursive programs.

A frequently used technique consists in solving the sub-problems in order of increasing size, the results of each sub-problem being kept in a table to avoid having to recalculate them. This technique, of which an example will be seen in section 6.5, is traditionally called 'dynamic programming'. (Note: These words are here given a meaning which is not their usual meaning in computer science.)

5.2. Example 1 Drawing a figure within a figure

Suppose we wish to draw the following pattern:

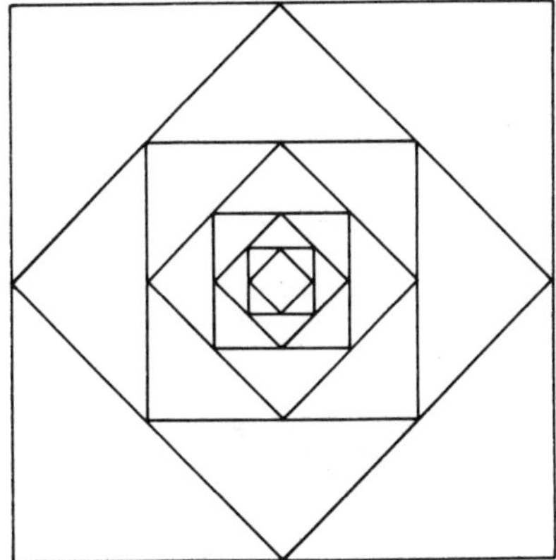

with equipment consisting of a sheet of paper, and a pen manipulated with the aid of two primitives:

> *place*(x, y) which positions the pen on the coordinates (x, y).
> *trace*(x, y) which traces the line-segment connecting the position of the pen to the coordinates (x, y). The pen is afterwards positioned at point(x, y).

We will not be concerned with the size of the sheet of paper, supposing it to be arbitrarily large.

Let P_n $(n \geqslant 0)$ be a drawing which reproduces the pattern n times. The above figure represents P_4. If $n \geqslant 1$, P_n can be decomposed into P_1 and P_{n-1}. This decomposition of P_n can be implemented in two different ways, according to whether P_1 is viewed as the largest or smallest pattern of P_n. We shall choose the first case, but the second would lead to an equally interesting program.

The meaning of P_1 and P_{n-1} being fixed, it remains to determine the method of tracing P_n. To minimize movement of the pen, we shall execute the drawing *without lifting the pen off the paper* and without going over any line twice. This implies:

> The pen comes back to its starting point having traced P_n ($n \geqslant 1$), since the degree of each vertex of the drawing is even. It is simpler to choose the same position for this starting point for every drawing P_n. A different solution would in fact require a supplementary parameter to specify the starting point.
>
> The starting and finishing point of the pen for P_{n-1} is on a point of P_1. It therefore has to be one of the vertices of the biggest square of P_{n-1}. We shall take the upper left vertex as an arbitrary starting point for tracing P_n.

These constraints mean that we have to begin with P_1, but have to trace all of P_{n-1} before finishing P_1. We have to:

(1) trace the segments of P_1 which connect the starting point of P_1 to the starting point of P_{n-1},

(2) trace P_{n-1},

(3) finish tracing P_1 by joining up the starting point of P_{n-1} to the starting point of P_1.

Finally, we have to find a way of tracing P_1 without lifting the pen off the paper and without going over any line twice, starting from the upper left vertex. We arbitrarily adopt the following approach:

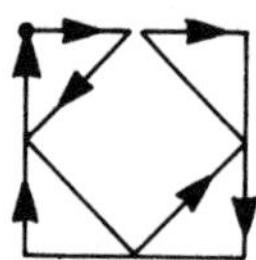

We therefore obtain the following recursive procedure (where x and y are the coordinates of the starting point of the drawing, and l is the length of a side of the largest square):

```
procedure draw (real value x,y,l; integer value n);
if n > 0 then
begin
   trace(x+l/2, y);
   trace(x+l/4,y−l/4);
   draw(x+l/4,y−l/4,l/2,n−1);
   trace(x,y−l/2);
   trace(x+l/2,y−l); trace(x+l,y−l/2); trace(x+l/2,y);
   trace(x+l,y);
   trace(x+l,y−l); trace(x,y−l); trace(x,y)
end
```

A principal call of procedure draw will be preceded by an execution of the primitive place to position the pen on the starting point of the drawing.

Analysis of procedure draw
Let us determine the total length of the lines of the drawing D, which is a function of l and n.

We have:

$$D(l,n) = 4l + 2l\sqrt{2} + D\left(\frac{l}{2}, n-1\right) \qquad \text{if } n > 0$$

$$D(l,0) = 0$$

It follows that:

$$D(l,n) = (4l + 2l\sqrt{2})\left(1 + \frac{1}{2} + \frac{1}{4} + \ldots + \frac{1}{2^{n-1}}\right)$$

$$D(l,n) = 4l(2 + \sqrt{2})\left(1 - \frac{1}{2^n}\right)$$

It is easy to see that, as n approaches infinity, $D(l,n)$ approaches $4l(2 + \sqrt{2})$.

5.3. Example 2 Binary search

5.3.1. Writing a recursive procedure for binary search

Suppose $T(1::n)$ is an array of n integers ($n \geqslant 1$) such that $T(i) < T(i+1)$ for all i, $1 \leqslant i < n$.

Given some integer k, we have to determine an integer i for which $T(i) \leqslant k < T(i+1)$. So as to cope with the cases $k<T(1)$ and $k \geqslant T(n)$, we can suppose $T(0) = -\infty$ and $T(n+1) = +\infty$. We then have $0 \leqslant i \leqslant n$.

Let this problem be denoted by $P_{1,n}$.

In order to give a recursive decomposition, we shall have to consider a more general problem $P_{inf,sup}$, where inf and sup are two integers such that $0 \leqslant inf-1 \leqslant sup \leqslant$ n. This is:
Let k be an integer such that $T(inf-1) \leqslant k \leqslant T(sup+1)$. Find integer i, $inf-1 \leqslant i \leqslant sup$, such that $T(i) \leqslant k < T(i+1)$. To solve $P_{inf,sup}$ by binary search, we use the following decomposition:

if $inf \leqslant sup$, let $l = \left\lfloor \dfrac{inf + sup}{2} \right\rfloor$.

if $k<T(l)$, then $T(inf-1) \leqslant k < T(l)$ and we only have to solve problem $P_{inf,l-1}$.
if $k \geqslant T(l)$, then $T(l) \leqslant k < T(sup+1)$ and we only have to solve problem $P_{l+1,sup}$.

if $inf > sup$, then $inf-1=sup$, and the solution is immediate:
the integer we are looking for is $i=sup=inf-1$.

Proving the partial correctness of this decomposition is easy. To prove termination, let us take $sup-inf+2$ as a measure of the size of the problem. If

$sup-inf+2=1$, the problem is solved directly. If $sup-inf+2>1$, we will have to solve either $P_{inf,l-1}$, which is of size $l-inf+1<sup-inf+2$, or $P_{l+1,sup}$, which is of size $sup-l+1<sup-inf+2$. The size of the sub-problem being dealt with recursively is therefore always strictly less than $sup-inf+2$, and this ensures termination.

Hence we have the following binary search procedure:

```
procedure chop1 (integer value inf,sup,k; integer variable i);
if inf > sup then i:=sup
else begin
     integer l;
     l:=(inf+sup) div 2;
     if k < T(l) then chop1 (inf, l-1,k,i)
     else chop1 (l+1,sup,k,i)
end
```

We shall make two modifications to this procedure, on the basis of the following remarks:

- parameter i can be used to store the value of $\left\lfloor \dfrac{inf+sup}{2} \right\rfloor$,

  and so we can dispense with variable l;

- if $k = T\left(\left\lfloor \dfrac{inf+sup}{2} \right\rfloor\right)$, the value we are looking for is $\left\lfloor \dfrac{inf+sup}{2} \right\rfloor$

  and it is then pointless to call the procedure recursively.

We thus obtain the following procedure:

```
procedure chop (integer value inf,sup,k; integer variable i);
if inf > sup then i:= sup
else begin
     i:=(inf+sup) div 2;
     if k < T(i) then chop (inf,i-1,sup,k,i)
     else if k > T(i) then chop (i+1,sup,k,i)
end
```

5.3.2. Formal proof of procedure chop

5.3.2.1. *Proof of partial correctness*

We have to prove the following statement:

(1) $(T(inf-1) \leqslant k < T(sup+1))\ \&$
$((inf-1 \leqslant j \leqslant sup) \rightarrow (T(j)<T(j+1))\ \&\ (inf-1 \leqslant sup)$
$\{Q\}$
$T(i) \leqslant k < T(i+1)$

where Q is the body of procedure *chop*.

For the sake of simplicity, we have not indicated in the postcondition that array T is not modified by execution of Q. This fact, which is obvious anyway, will therefore not be proved formally.

We assume by the induction hypothesis that the two recursive calls are correct, that is to say that

$(T(inf-1) \leqslant k < T(i))$ & $((inf-1 \leqslant j \leqslant i-1) \rightarrow T(j) < T(j+1)))$ & $(inf-1 \leqslant i-1)$
$\{chop(inf, i-1, k, i)\}$
$T(i) \leqslant k < T(i+1)$

and

$(T(i) \leqslant k < T(sup+1))$ & $((i \leqslant j \leqslant sup) \rightarrow (T(j) < T(j+1)))$ & $(i \leqslant sup)$
$\{chop(i+1, sup, k, i)\}$
$T(i) \leqslant k < T(i+1)$

Remark

The calls $chop(inf, i-1, k, i)$ and $chop(i+1, sup, k, i)$ do not satisfy condition (v) of section 3.4.2 (since the actual variable parameter i appears as an operand of the actual value parameters). The above statements are nevertheless correct, as the formal value parameters *inf* and *sup* do not appear in the postcondition $T(i) \leqslant k < T(i+1)$.

Let us denote the precondition of (1) by E. To prove (1), it is sufficient to show

(2) E & $(inf > sup)$
  $\{i := sup\}$
  $T(i) \leqslant k < T(i+1)$

and

(3) E & $(inf \leqslant sup)$
  {**begin** $i := (inf+sup)$ **div** 2 ;
   if $k < T(i)$ **then** $chop(inf, i-1, k, i)$
   else if $k > T(i)$ **then** $chop(i+1, sup, k, i)$
  end}
  $T(i) \leqslant k < T(i+1)$

Proof of (2)

E & $(inf > sup) \sim E$ & $(inf = sup+1) \rightarrow (T(sup) \leqslant k < T(sup+1))$

and also

$T(sup) \leqslant k < T(sup+1)$
$\{i := sup\}$
$T(i) \leqslant k < T(i+1)$

Proof of (3)

Let E_1 denote the assertion

  $T(inf-1) \leqslant k)$ & $((inf-1 \leqslant j \leqslant i-1) \rightarrow (T(j) < T(j+1)))$ & $(inf \leqslant i)$

and E_2 the assertion

  $(k < T(sup+1))$ & $(i \leqslant j \leqslant sup) \rightarrow (T(j) < T(j+1)))$ & $(i \leqslant sup)$

We have (induction hypothesis):

E_1 & $(k<T(i))$ $\{chop(inf,i-1,k,i)\}$ $T(i) \leqslant k < T(i+1)$

E_2 & $(k>T(i))$ $\{chop(i+1,sup,k,i)\}$ $T(i) \leqslant k < T(i+1)$

Furthermore:

$(T(i)<T(i+1))$ & $(k=T(i)) \rightarrow (T(i) \leqslant k < T(i+1))$

Now

E_1 & $E_2 \rightarrow E_1$, E_1 & $E_2 \rightarrow E_2$ and E_1 & $E_2 \rightarrow T(i)<T(i+1)$

It follows that:

E_1 & E_2 & $(k<T(i))$ $\{chop(inf,i-1,k,i)\}$ $T(i) \leqslant k < T(i+1)$

E_1 & E_2 & $(k>T(i))$ $\{chop(i+1,sup,k,i)\}$ $T(i) \leqslant k < T(i+1)$

E_1 & E_2 & $(k=T(i)) \rightarrow (T(i) \leqslant k < T(i+1))$

Hence:

E_1 & E_2

{*if* $k < T(i)$ **then** $chop(inf, i-1,k,i)$

else if $k > T(i)$ **then** $chop(i+1,sup,k,i)$}

$T(i) \leqslant k < T(i+1)$

Now

E_1 & $E_2 \sim (T(inf-1) \leqslant k < T(sup+1))$ &

$((inf-1 \leqslant j \leqslant sup) \rightarrow (T(j)<t(j+1)))$ & $(inf \leqslant i \leqslant sup)$

Finally, we have:

$(T(inf-1) \leqslant k < T(sup+1))$ &

$((inf-1 \leqslant j \leqslant sup) \rightarrow (T(j)<T(j+1)))$ & $\left(inf \leqslant \left\lfloor \frac{inf+sup}{2} \right\rfloor \leqslant sup\right)$

$\{i:=(inf+sup)$ **div** $2\}$

$(T(inf-1) \leqslant k < T(sup+1))$ &

$((inf-1 \leqslant j \leqslant sup) \rightarrow (T(j)<T(j+1)))$ & $(inf \leqslant i \leqslant sup)$

The precondition is equivalent to E & $(inf \leqslant sup)$, which completes the proof of (3).

We have thus proved (1), that is to say that the body of procedure *chop* is correct. In particular, for the principal call $chop(1, n, k, i)$, we have the following precondition:

$(T(0) \leqslant k < T(n+1)$ & $((0 \leqslant j \leqslant n) \rightarrow (T(j)<T(j+1)))$ & $(0 \leqslant n)$

With the convention $T(0) = -\infty$ and $T(n+1) = +\infty$, this is equivalent to

$((1 \leqslant j \leqslant n-1) \rightarrow (T(j)<T(j+1)))$ & $(n \geqslant 0)$

Remark

Array T has been defined with bounds 1 and n. This definition does not have to be modified. In fact, $T(0)$ and $T(n+1)$ only appear in the conditions; procedure *chop* does not make use of them.

5.3.2.2. *Proof of termination*

Consider the function $v : W_E \times X_E \rightarrow \mathbb{N}$, whose value is $sup-inf+1$. For there to be a recursive call, it must be the case that $inf \leqslant sup$.

Then $inf \leqslant \lfloor (inf+sup)/2 \rfloor \leqslant sup$, which implies:

$$\left\lfloor \frac{inf+sup}{2} \right\rfloor - inf < sup+1-inf, \text{ and } sup - \left\lfloor \frac{inf+sup}{2} \right\rfloor < sup-inf+1.$$

Consequently, the value of v is strictly decreasing each time we pass from a call of *chop* to an embedded recursive call, ensuring the termination of procedure *chop*.

5.3.3. Analysis

Let $d(n)$ be the execution time of procedure *chop*, where n is the number of elements in the array, i.e. $n = sup-inf+1$. To analyse $d(n)$, we must compute the execution times of the calls $chop(inf,i-1,k,i)$ and $chop(i+1,sup,k,i)$, with $i = \lfloor (inf+sup)/2 \rfloor$, or in other words:

$$d\left(\left\lfloor \frac{inf+sup}{2} \right\rfloor - inf\right) = d\left(\left\lfloor \frac{n-1}{2} \right\rfloor\right)$$

and

$$d\left(sup - \left\lfloor \frac{inf+sup}{2} \right\rfloor\right) = d\left(\left\lfloor \frac{n}{2} \right\rfloor\right).$$

We therefore obtain a recurrence relation between $d(n)$ and the two values $d(\lfloor (n-1)/2 \rfloor)$ and $d(\lfloor n/2 \rfloor)$. This relation can be simplified if at each step of the recurrence (corresponding to a new call of procedure *chop*), we have $\lfloor (n-1)/2 \rfloor = \lfloor n/2 \rfloor$.

This equality is satisfied if and only if n is odd.

On the other hand, $d(1)$ can be calculated immediately.

This leads to a solution of the recurrence relation for the values of n: 3, 7, 15, $\ldots, 2^m-1, \ldots$

Let $d_m = d(2^m-1)$. The recurrence relation will then express d_m as a function of d_{m-1}.

The case where n is not of the form 2^m-1 is discussed in section 5.3.3.2.

5.3.3.1. *Analysis of* d_m, $(m>0)$

Let a be the execution time of parameter passing and the test $inf>sup$,
b the execution time of $i:=(inf+sup)$ **div** 2 and the test $k<T(i)$,
c the execution time of the test $k>T(i)$,
e the execution time of $i:=sup$.

Unfortunately, d_m cannot be expressed only as a function of d_{m-1}, a, b, c, and e. It also depends on the relationship between the value of k and the elements in the given array T. It would be possible to calculate all values of d_m, corresponding to the various cases. But we will be satisfied with a general result and compute only the average execution time $\overline{d_m}$, i.e. the average of the different values of d_m, weighted according to the probability of their appearance.

Suppose value k has a probability p_1 of being among the elements of T (and so a probability $p_2=1-p_1$ of not being in T), and that each value of T is equally likely to be k. In other words,

$$\text{if } inf \leqslant j \leqslant sup, \qquad \Pr(k=T(j)) = \frac{p_1}{n}$$

$$\text{if } inf-1 \leqslant j \leqslant sup, \qquad \Pr(T(j)<k<T(j+1)) = \frac{p_2}{n+1}$$

Under this assumption we have, in the case $sup-inf+1 = n = 2^m-1$:

$$\Pr\left(k<T\left(\left\lfloor\frac{inf+sup}{2}\right\rfloor\right)\right) = Pr\left(k>T\left(\left\lfloor\frac{inf+sup}{2}\right\rfloor\right)\right)$$

$$= \frac{1}{2}\left(1-\Pr\left(k=T\left(\left\lfloor\frac{inf+sup}{2}\right\rfloor\right)\right)\right)$$

$$= \frac{1}{2}\left(1-\frac{p_1}{2^m-1}\right)$$

$$1 - Pr\left(k<T\left(\left\lfloor\frac{inf+sup}{2}\right\rfloor\right)\right) = \frac{1}{2}\left(1+\frac{p_1}{2^m-1}\right)$$

Hence the equation ($m \geqslant 1$):

$$\overline{d_m} = a + b + \overline{d_{m-1}} \cdot \frac{1}{2}\left(1-\frac{p_1}{2^m-1}\right) + c \cdot \frac{1}{2}\left(1+\frac{p_1}{2^m-1}\right) + \overline{d_{m-1}} \cdot \frac{1}{2}\left(1-\frac{p_1}{2^m-1}\right)$$

From this we deduce the following system:

$$(0) \quad \overline{d_m} = a + b + \frac{c}{2}\left(1+\frac{p_1}{2^m-1}\right) + \left(1-\frac{p_1}{2^m-1}\right)\overline{d_{m-1}}$$

$$\ldots$$

$$(l) \quad \overline{d_{m-1}} = a + b + \frac{c}{2}\left(1+\frac{p_1}{2^{m-l}-1}\right) + \left(1-\frac{p_1}{2^{m-l}-1}\right) \text{——}$$

$$\ldots$$

$$(m-1)\,\overline{\mathrm{d}_1} = a + b + \frac{c}{2}(1+p_1) + (1-p_1)\overline{d_0}$$

$$= a + b + \frac{c}{2}(1+p_1) + (a+e)\,(1-p_1) \text{ since } \overline{d_0} = a+e.$$

Suppose, for $l = 1, 2, \ldots, m-1$,

$$\alpha_l = \prod_{h=0}^{l-1}\left(1-\frac{p_1}{2^{m-h}-1}\right)$$

and $\alpha_0 = 1$.

Multiply each equation by the corresponding coefficient α_l:

$$(l)\ \alpha_l\ \overline{d_{m-l}} = (a+b)\alpha_l + \frac{c}{2}\left(1 + \frac{p_1}{2^{m-l}-1}\right)\alpha_l + \alpha_{l+1}\ \overline{d_{m-l-1}}$$

This leads to:

$$\overline{d_m} = (a+e)\ (1-p_1)\alpha_{m-1} + (a+b)\sum_{l=0}^{m-1}\alpha_l + \frac{c}{2}\sum_{l=0}^{m-1}\alpha_l\left(1 + \frac{p_1}{2^{m-l}-1}\right)$$

where $\alpha_l = \prod_{h=0}^{l-1}\left(1 - \frac{p_1}{2^{m-h}-1}\right)$ and $\alpha_0 = 1$.

5.3.3.2. *Analysis of $\overline{d(n)}$*

From the definition of α_l, we deduce:

$$1 - 2^{l-m} \leqslant \alpha_l \leqslant 1$$

Hence:

$$m - 1 \leqslant \sum_{l=0}^{m-1}\alpha_l \leqslant m$$

On the other hand:

$$1 \leqslant 1 + \frac{p_1}{2^{m-l}-1} \leqslant 2$$

We therefore obtain the inequalities:

$$(m-1)\ (a+b) + \frac{c}{2}(m-1) \leqslant \overline{d_m} \leqslant a+e+m(a+b)+mc$$

$$(m-1)\left(a+b + \frac{c}{2}\right) \leqslant \overline{d_m} \leqslant m(a+b+c)+a+e.$$

It follows that $\overline{d_m}$ is of order m.

Under the hypotheses of the last section, function $\overline{d(n)}$ is non-decreasing. Thus, if $2^{m-1}-1 < n < 2^m-1$, we have $\overline{d_{m-1}} \leqslant \overline{d(n)} \leqslant \overline{d_m}$. Consequently, procedure *chop* has an average execution time of order $(\log n)$.

5.3.3.3. *Particular cases*

(1) If $p_1 = 0$, value k has a null probability of occurring in array T. In this case, we find $\alpha_l = 1$, for all l, and

$$\overline{d_m} = a+e+m\left(a+b+\frac{c}{2}\right).$$

(2) If $p_1 = 1$, value k will be in array T, so that

$$\alpha_l = \prod_{h=0}^{l-1} \frac{2^{m-h}-2}{2^{m-h}-1} = \prod_{h=0}^{l-1} \frac{2(2^{m-(h+1)}-1)}{2^{m-h}-1} = 2^l \frac{2^{m-l}-1}{2^m-1}$$

and $\sum_{l=0}^{m-1} \alpha_l = \frac{1}{2^m-1} \sum_{l=0}^{m-1} (2^m-2^l) = m-1 + \frac{m}{2^m-1}$

This gives:

$$\overline{d_m} = m\left(a+b+\frac{c}{2}\right) - (a+b) + \frac{m}{2^m-1}\left(a+b+\frac{c}{2}\right)$$

5.3.3.4. *Variant*

Consider the procedure *chop2*, derived from *chop* by eliminating the test $k > T(i)$. The recursive call *chop2*(i+1, *sup*, k, i) is then executed if $k \geqslant T(i)$.

Let d'_m be the execution time of *chop2* for an array with 2^m-1 elements. Using the same notations as before, we have:

$$d'_m = a + b + d'_{m-1} \qquad m \geqslant 1$$
$$d'_0 = a + e$$

Remark

d'_m is independent of k, unlike d_m.

From the recurrence relation, we deduce:

$$d'_m = m(a+b) + a + e$$

Procedure *chop2* is therefore more efficient than procedure chop whenever k is not in array T.

Let us compare $\overline{d_m}$ and d'_m when k is not in array T.

Suppose $a = 6$, $b = 4$, $c = 2$, and $e = 1$. We then have:

$$\overline{d_m} = 11m - 10 + 11\frac{m}{2^m-1} = 11m\left(1 + \frac{1}{2^m-1}\right) - 10$$

$$d'_m = 10m + 7$$

The conclusion is that procedure *chop* is faster than procedure *chop2* for $m < 17$, or $n < 2^{17}$. The fact that *chop2* is asymptotically more efficient than *chop* is therefore of no practical interest.

5.4. Example 3 Sorting by partitioning ('quicksort')

5.4.1. The sort algorithm

Sorting an array consists in arranging its elements in a given order. We shall suppose that the array to be sorted, $A(1::N)$, is an array of integers whose elements have to be arranged in order of increasing size.

Let i and j be such that $1 \leqslant i, j \leqslant N$, and let $A(i::j)$ denote the sub-array of A from index i to index j inclusive.

Consider the problem $P_{inf,sup}$: 'sort $A(inf::sup)$'.

Sorting by partitioning is based on the following recursive decomposition:

if $inf \geqslant sup$, $A(inf::sup)$ is either empty or a single element, and therefore sorted.

if $inf < sup$,

(1) begin by permuting the elements of $A(inf::sup)$, until an index i is found such that:

$A(l) \leqslant A(i)$ for all l, $inf \leqslant l < i$

$A(i) \leqslant A(m)$ for all m, $i < m \leqslant sup$.

Denoting the value of $A(i)$ by k, this property can be represented as follows:

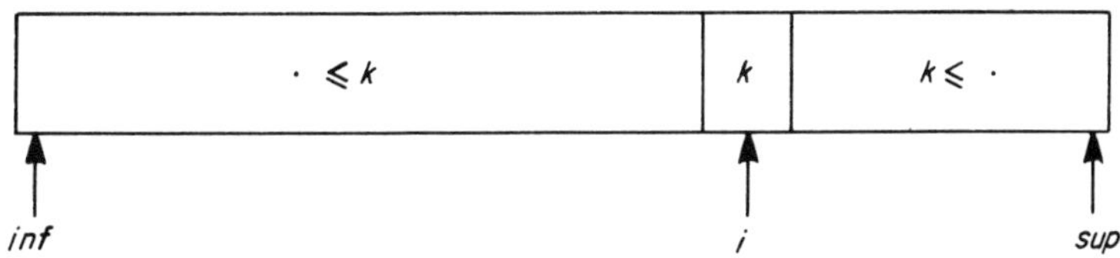

We shall call this stage: 'partitioning' of $A(inf::sup)$.

(2) In the sorted array, the element with index i will have value k. After partitioning, all that is necessary is to solve the two problems $P_{inf,i-1}$ and $P_{i+1,sup}$.

From this decomposition we deduce the following recursive procedure:

```
procedure sort (integer value inf, sup) ;
if inf < sup then
   begin integer i ;
      partition (inf,sup,i) ;
      sort (inf,i−1) ; sort (i+1,sup)
   end
```

5.4.2. Constructing the partitioning procedure

The partitioning procedure applies to $A(inf::sup)$, with $inf < sup$. The postcondition of the partitioning is:

there exists i_0 such that

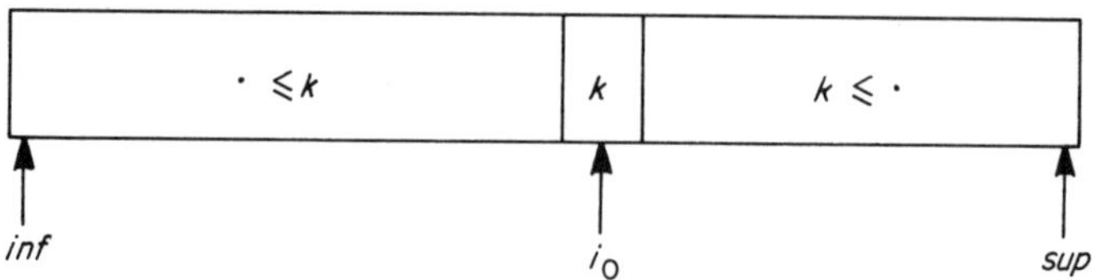

This postcondition can be satisfied by any value k appearing in $A(inf::sup)$. We can therefore choose arbitrarily some value k among the elements of $A(inf::sup)$ before partitioning. This value k will be called the 'pivot' of the partitioning. We shall take $k = A(inf)$. This choice is discussed in section 5.4.4(b) and (c).

The postcondition is similar to that of the 'three-coloured flag' (see §2.2.1). The following loop invariant will be used:

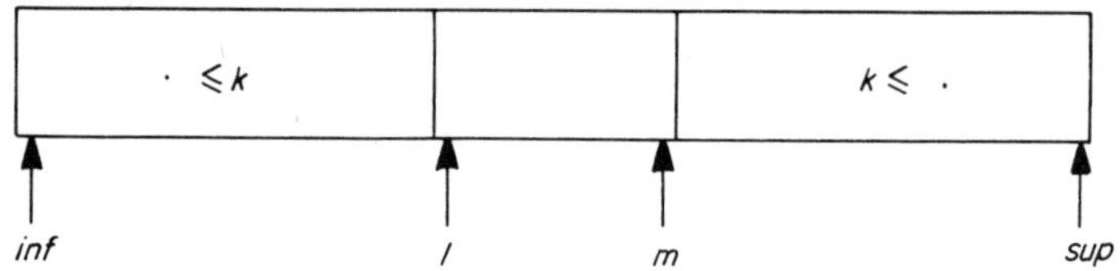

that is to say

$$(inf \leqslant l \leqslant m \leqslant sup) \ \& \ (inf \leqslant j < l \rightarrow (A(j) \leqslant k)) \ \&$$
$$(m < j \leqslant sup \rightarrow (A(j) \geqslant k))$$

To reduce the number of exchanges, let us construct a loop similar to that of program (I(b)) for the three-coloured flag. We obtain:

```
(1)    while l ≤ m do
          if A(l) ≤ k then l := l +1
          else begin
(2)         while (A(m) > k) and (l < m) do m := m − 1 ;
            A(l) :=: A(m) ;
            m := m − 1
          end
```

Termination of loop (2) is ensured by the test $A(m) > k$, as we have chosen $k = A(inf)$. The test $l < m$ must, however, be computed after this loop, the partitioning being complete if we have $l > m$.

On the other hand, after exchanging $A(l)$ and $A(m)$, we have $A(l) \leqslant k$, and so l can be increased by 1.

The postcondition of the loop is:

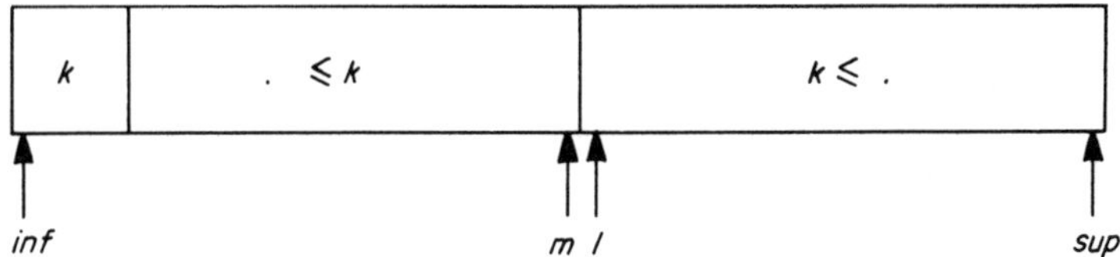

To obtain the postcondition of the partitioning, we simply swap values $A(inf)$ and $A(m)$.

Hence the following procedure:

```
procedure partition (integer value inf,sup ; integer variable m;
begin integer l,k ;
   l := inf + 1 ; m := sup ; k := A(inf) ;
   while l ≤ m do
     if A(l) ≤ k then l := l + 1
     else begin
         while A(m) > k do m := m - 1 ;
         if l < m then
           begin
             A(l) := A(m) ;
             m := m - 1 ;
             l := l + 1
           end
         end ;
     A(m) :=:A(inf)
end
```

Exercise 1
Consider the procedure:

```
procedure partition1 (integer value inf,sup ; integer variable m)
begin integer l,k ;
   l := inf + 1 ; m := sup ; k := A(inf) ;
   LOOP while A(l) < k do l := l + 1 ;
          while A(m) > k do m := m - 1 ;
          if l < m then
            begin A(l) :=: A(m) ; l := l + 1 ; m := m - 1 ;
                  goto LOOP
            end ;
   A(m) :=: A(inf)
end
```

Show that the procedure *partition*1 is correct for array $A(inf::sup)$ if $A(sup + 1)$ is defined, and greater than or equal to $A(inf)$.

Suppose procedure *sort* of section 5.4.1 uses procedure *partition*1, and let $A(1::N)$ be the array to be sorted.

Show that *sort* will be correct if $A(N + 1)$ is defined, and greater than or equal to all the elements of A.

Exercise 2

Consider the procedure:

```
procedure partition2 (integer value inf,sup ; integer variable m) ;
begin integer l,k ;
   l := inf ; m := sup ; k := A(inf) ;
   LOOP: while A(m) > k do m := m - 1 ;
            A(l) :=: A(m) ; l := l + 1 ;
            while A(l) < k do l := l + 1 ;
            if l < m then
              begin A(l) :=: A(m) ; m := m - 1 ;
                     goto LOOP
              end
end
```

(a) Show that:
   at the label LOOP, condition $A(l) = k$ always holds.
   when test $l < m$ is executed, condition $A(m) = k$ always holds.

(b) Deduce another form of the same procedure, where swaps are replaced by assignments. Show that this transformation is only correct if array A satisfies the same condition as in the previous exercise.

(c) Compare the operations executed by the procedures *partition*1 and *partition*2 when it has been modified in this way.

5.4.3. Analysis of sorting by partitioning

We shall not discuss the analysis of space requirements (but see exercise 6.3.2.3(2)).

5.4.3.1. *Analysis of the partitioning procedure* (§5.4.2)

Suppose $n = sup - inf + 1$.

(i) Variables l and m are initialized to $inf+1$ and sup, respectively. They are modified only by the assignments $l{:=}l+1$ and $m{:=}m-1$, and at the end of the partitioning phase, we have $l = m+1$.

   The number of assignments to l or m is therefore equal to $sup-inf$, which is $n-1$. Hence the execution time of procedure partition is order n at best.

(ii) Let n_1 be the number of executions of the loop '**while** $l \leqslant m$', and n_2 the number of executions of the loop '**while** $A(m)>k$'. It can be shown that:

$n_1 + n_2 \leqslant n$

execution time of the loop '**while** $l \leqslant m$' is less than or equal to $an_1 + bn_2$, where a and b are independent of n.

The execution time of procedure partition is therefore order n at worst.

It follows from (i) and (ii) that procedure partition has an execution time of order n.

The exact value of this execution time depends on the arrangement of elements in array A: in particular, the number of exchanges varies from 1 (in an already sorted array, for example) to $\lfloor (n+1)/2 \rfloor$. It is simpler to analyse just the number of comparisons between elements in the array. This is the normal criterion of complexity for sorting algorithms. The partitioning procedure makes $n-1$, n, or $n+1$ comparisons with the pivot k. Procedure partition1 (exercise 1, §5.4.2) makes exactly $n+1$ comparisons.

Exercise

For partitioning to be achieved, the pivot needs only to be compared once with each of the $n-1$ other elements. Why then do the procedures we have just described execute redundant comparisons? What tests on the indices l and m have to be added for these procedures to execute exactly $n-1$ comparisons with the pivot? Are the procedures obtained more efficient, in execution time, than the initial procedures?

5.4.3.2. *Analysis of procedure sort* (§5.4.1)

We analyse the number of comparisons made by procedure sort, assuming that the partitioning procedure being used makes exactly $n-1$ comparisons (see the exercise below).

Let i_0 be the value of i after partitioning and let $t = i_0 - inf + 1$.

The first recursive call sorts an array A_G with $t-1$ elements, and the second an array A_D with $n-t$ elements. We will indicate the number of comparisons needed to sort array A with n elements by $K(n,A)$. We have:

$$K(0,A) = K(1,A) = 0$$

$$K(n,A) = n-1 + K(t-1,A_G) + K(n-t,A_D), \qquad \text{if } n > 1.$$

The value of $K(n,A)$ depends not only on n, but also on the arrangement of elements in array A, which determines the value of t. In certain cases, the sub-arrays A_G and A_D are close in size (when t is close to $n/2$). In other cases, their sizes can be very different (for instance, when $t=1$ or $t=n$).

We saw in section 5.1 how the decomposition of a problem into sub-problems of equal size leads to efficient programs. The result of partitioning will therefore be more beneficial if the sizes of the two sub-arrays are close. We shall first analyse sorting in the best case (when each partitioning produces two sub-arrays of equal size), and in the worst case (when each

partitioning produces an empty sub-array). We shall then analyse the average value of $K(n,A)$, assuming that all cases are equiprobable.
(Note: Since only the order of elements in A, and not their value, is relevant, we shall assume in what follows that the elements in A are integers in the range 1 to N.)

(a) *Best case*
This is obtained when, for each call of procedure *sort*, partitioning divides A into two sub-arrays of equal size. This happens, for instance, with the seven-element array (4, 2, 5, 3, 6, 1, 7). It is easy to check that for such a partition to be possible n must be of the form 2^m-1 $(m \geqslant 0)$.

The number of comparisons $K_{\text{min}}(n)$ for sorting the array is then given by the equations

$$K_{\text{min}}(0) = 0, \ K_{\text{min}}(1) = 0,$$
$$K_{\text{min}}(2^m-1) = 2^m - 2 + 2.K_{\text{min}}(2^{m-1}-1), \qquad m \geqslant 2$$

whose solution is

$$K_{\text{min}}(2^m-1) \times m2^m - 2^{m+1} + 2$$

or

$$K_{\text{min}}(n) = (m-2)n + m$$

The number of comparisons in sorting by partitioning is therefore order (n log n) in the best case.

(b) *Worst case*
This is obtained when, for each call of procedure *sort*, partitioning produces an empty sub-array. For example, with array $(1, 2, \ldots, N)$, the sub-arrays A_G are always empty; with array $(N, 1, 2, \ldots, N-1)$, the sub-arrays A_D are always empty.

Exercise
If the n elements to be sorted are all different, and $n \geqslant 2$, show that there are exactly 2^{n-1} worst cases.

The number of comparisons for sorting the array, $K_{\text{max}}(n)$, is then given by the equation

$$K_{\text{max}}(0) = 0, \ K_{\text{max}}(1) = 0,$$
$$K_{\text{max}}(n) = n-1 + K_{\text{max}}(n-1), \qquad n \geqslant 2$$

So

$$K_{\text{max}}(n) = \sum_{i=1}^{n-1} i = \frac{n(n-1)}{2}$$

The number of comparisons, for an array with n elements, is therefore order n^2 in the worst case.

(c) *Average case*
To simplify the analysis, we assume that all the elements of the array are different (see section 5.4.4(d)). If the array has n elements, there are $n!$

possible cases, namely the permutations of $\{1, 2, \ldots, n\}$. Our average case analysis will assume the hypothesis that *each of these n! cases has the same probability of occurrence.*

We are going to calculate $K(n)$, the average number of comparisons for sorting an array with n elements.

Let $K_j(n)$ be the average number of comparisons for sorting an array with n elements, the pivot $A(inf)$ being equal to j $(1 \leqslant j \leqslant n)$. According to the equiprobability assumption mentioned above, we have:

$$K(n) = \frac{1}{n}\,(K_1(n) + K_2(n) + \ldots + K_n(n)) \tag{1}$$

We have seen that, to sort an array A with n elements $(n > 1)$ and pivot j, the number of comparisons is:

$$K(n, A) = n-1 + K(j-1, A_G) + K(n-j, A_D) \tag{2}$$

The average value of $K(n, A)$ for the $(n-1)!$ possible configurations of the array is $K_j(n)$.

To calculate $K_j(n)$, it is therefore sufficient to calculate the average value of the second part of equation (2). This means analysing the probability of occurrence of each configuration of A_G and A_D.

Let c_1 be one of the $(j-1)!$ possible configurations of sub-array A_G. Denote by A_1 the set of configurations of A whose partitioning produces c_1.

Let c_2 be a configuration of A_G obtained by permuting two elements p and q in c_1, and A_2 the set of configurations of A whose partitioning produces c_2.

The sequence of operations performed by procedure partition is determined only by comparison of the elements in the array with the pivot. Consequently, as elements p and q are both smaller than the pivot, partitioning will execute the same operations for two configurations of A differing only by the permutation of elements p and q. It follows that, for each configuration of A_1 (respectively, A_2), the configuration obtained by permuting p and q produces c_2 (respectively, c_1) by partitioning, and therefore belongs to A_2 (respectively, A_1). The two sets A_1 and A_2 therefore have the same number of elements. The probabilities of occurrence of c_1 and c_2 are the sums of the probabilities of the elements of A_1 and A_2, respectively. The $(n-1)!$ possible cases for array A being equiprobable, the two configurations c_1 and c_2 are equiprobable.

We have thus proved that two configurations of A_G, which differ by the permutation of a pair of elements, are equiprobable. As a result, any two configurations of A_G are equiprobable, since we can always pass from one to the other through a sequence of permutations of pairs of elements. The same argument applies to sub-array A_D.

The average values of $K(j-1, A_G)$ and $K(n-j, A_D)$ are therefore $K(j-1)$ and $K(n-j)$.

According to (2), we therefore have:

$$K_j(n) = n-1 + K(j-1) + K(n-j), \qquad \textit{for } n>1.$$

Hence, according to equation (1):

$$K(n) = n-1 + \frac{1}{n}\left(\sum_{j=1}^{n} K(j-1) + \sum_{j=1}^{n} K(n-j) \right), \qquad n>1$$

or:

$$\boxed{\begin{array}{l} K(n) = n-1 + \dfrac{2}{n} \displaystyle\sum_{j=0}^{n-1} K(j) \\ K(0) = K(1) = 0 \end{array}}$$

with

Solution of the recurrence equation

The above equation can be written:

$$n\,K(n) = n(n-1) + 2 \sum_{j=0}^{n-1} K(j)$$

Hence:

$$(n-1)\,K(n-1) = (n-1)(n-2) + 2 \sum_{j=0}^{n-2} K(j)$$

From these two equalities we obtain by subtraction:

$$nK(n) - (n+1)\,K(n-1) = 2(n-1)$$

or equivalently:

$$\frac{K(n)}{n+1} - \frac{K(n-1)}{n} = \frac{2(n-1)}{n(n+1)}\,.$$

Assuming

$$x_n = \frac{K(n)}{n+1}$$

the recurrence equation becomes:

$$x_n - x_{n-1} = \frac{2(n-1)}{n(n+1)}$$

$$x_0 = x_1 = 0$$

The solution of this equation is:

$$x_n = \sum_{j=1}^{n} \frac{2(j-1)}{j(j+1)}$$

that is to say:

$$x_n = \sum_{j=1}^{n} \frac{2}{j} - \sum_{j=1}^{n} \left(\frac{4}{j} - \frac{4}{j+1} \right)$$

$$x_n = 2 \sum_{j=1}^{n} \frac{1}{j} - 4 + \frac{4}{n+1}$$

From this we deduce:

$$K(n) = 2(n+1) \sum_{j=1}^{n} \frac{1}{j} - 4n$$

$$K(0) = K(1) = 0$$

Now, according to Euler's formula, the harmonic number

$$H_n = \sum_{j=1}^{n} \frac{1}{j}$$

is equal to $\ln(n) + \gamma + \epsilon$ (where γ is Euler's constant and ϵ approaches zero when n approaches infinity). The average number of comparisons is therefore of order $(n \log n)$.

Remark
The higher order terms of $K_{\min}(n)$ and $K(n)$ are $n \log_2(n)$ and $2n \ln(n)$ respectively.

The quotient $\dfrac{K(n)}{K_{\min}(n)}$ therefore approaches $2\ln(2)$, or 1.386 . . . .

The average number of comparisons is therefore very close to the number of comparisons in the best case.

5.4.4. Notes

(a) We have seen that the execution time for partitioning is order n, the same as the number of comparisons. From this we can deduce that sorting by partitioning has an execution time of order $(n \log n)$ in the best and average cases, and order n^2 in the worst case. A more complete analysis would show that the average execution time is close to the execution time in the best case, and that the variance in execution time is small (which is why execution times are generally close to the average time).

(b) The above average case analysis is correct providing that the hypothesis of equiprobability is true. If it is not, then the existence of worst cases, with execution times of order n^2, prevents us from coming to any conclusions as to the average efficiency of the algorithm. However, if we modify the partitioning in such a way that the pivot is chosen at random from among the elements in the array to be partitioned, then our average case analysis is correct.

(c) We have seen that the best cases correspond to a partitioning of the array into two sub-arrays of the same size. This is achieved when the value of the pivot is the median element in the array. The average execution time can be improved if we estimate the median element using a sample of 3 elements in the array, and make this the pivot.

(d) In the case where elements in the array can be equal, the results of the average case analysis remain valid, as long as the number of elements in the array is considerably smaller than the number of their possible values. But of course, when this is the case, the probability of equal elements appearing is low.

(e) For small arrays of less than 10 elements, sorting by partitioning is less efficient than sorting by insertion, for instance. It is therefore preferable, in procedure sort, to replace the test $inf < sup$ by a test $inf < sup - 10$. Ordering the array can then be completed with the help of sorting by insertion.

(f) To obtain a more efficient sorting procedure, we can:

— replace the call of procedure partition by the corresponding sequence of instructions,

— eliminate recursion (see Chapter 6.3).

5.5. Example 4 Drawing triangles

This example makes use of the drawing primitives defined in section 5.2.

5.5.1. A non-optimal procedure

Consider the following procedure:

```
procedure triangles1 (real value x, y, d, h) ;
if y + d < h then
   begin
      trace (x-d, y+d) ;
      triangles1 (x-d, y+d, d, h) ;
      trace (x+d, y+d) ;
      triangles1 (x+d, y+d, d, h) ;
      trace (x,y)
   end
```

The sequence *place*(x, y) ; *triangles*1(x, y, d, h), where d is strictly positive, produces the following drawing:

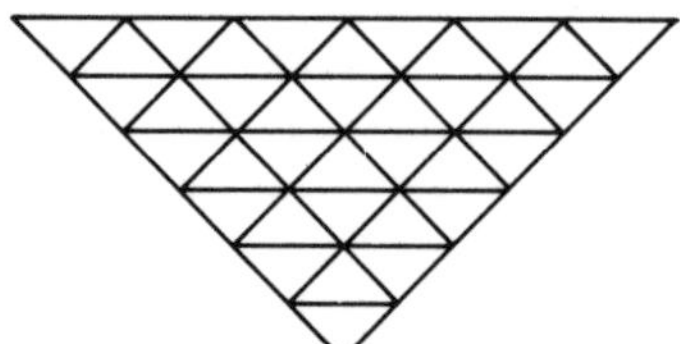

Analysis of the procedure triangles1

Let *triangles*(x, y, d, h) be called with $d > 0$. The number of executions of the primitive *trace* for this call is a function T_1 of y, d, and h satisfying:

$$T_1(y,d,h) = 3+2.T_1\ (y+d,\ d,\ h) \qquad \text{if } y+d < h$$
$$T_1(y,d,h) = 0 \qquad \text{if } y+d \geqslant h$$

From this it follows that:

$$T_1(y,d,h) = 3+2.T_1(y+d,d,h) \qquad y+d < h$$
$$2.T_1(y+d,d,h) = 2\times 3 + 2^2.T_1(y+2d,d,h) \qquad y+2d < h$$
$$\vdots \qquad\qquad \vdots$$
$$2^k.T_1(y+d,d,h) = 2^k \times 3 + 2^{k+1}.T_1(y+(k+1)d,d,h) \quad y+(k+1)d < h$$
$$2^{k+1}.T_1(y+(k+1)d,d,h) = 0 \qquad y+(k+2)d \geqslant h$$

Hence:

$$T_1(y,d,h) = 3.\sum_{i=0}^{k} 2^i = 3.(2^{k+1}-1), \text{ with } k \text{ such that}$$

$$y+(k+1)d < h \text{ and } y+(k+2)d \geqslant h.$$

This result, which is exponential in k, is obviously not optimal, since all the triangles of the figure with vertex $(x,\ y+2d)$ are drawn at least twice.

5.5.2. An optimal procedure

Let us replace the second recursive call of *triangles*1 by a call to a procedure *band*, which will draw only the part of the figure with vertex $(x+d,\ y+d)$ which has not yet been drawn, that is to say:

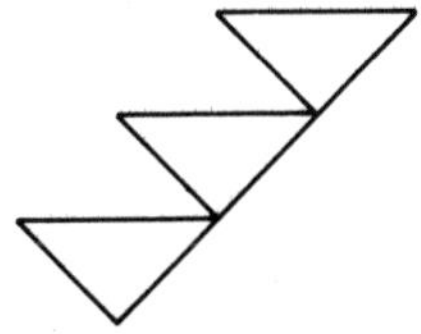

As an exercise, verify that the following procedure produces this drawing.

```
procedure band (real value x,y,d,h) ;
if y+d < h then
   begin
      trace (x-d,y+d) ;
      trace (x+d,y+d) ;
      band (x+d,y+d,d,h) ;
      trace (x,y)
   end
```

The following procedure *triangles*2 then produces the same drawing as *triangles*1 (the verification is again left as an exercise).

```
procedure triangles2 (real value x,y,d,h) ;
if y+d < h then
   begin
      trace (x-d,y+d) ;
      triangles2 (x-d,y+d,d,h) ;
      trace (x+d,y+d) ;
      band (x+d,y+d,d,h) ;
      trace (x,y)
   end
```

Analysis of procedure triangles2
Let *triangles*2(x,y,d,h) be called with $d > 0$, and let k be such that $y + (k+1)d < h \leqslant y + (k+2)d$.

(*Exercise*: Show that the number of executions of the primitive *trace* for the call *band*(x, y, d, h) is equal to $3(k+1)$. Let $T_2(y, d, h)$ be the number of calls of the primitive *trace*, for the call *triangles*2(x, y, d, h).

We have:

$$T_2(y, d, h) = 3 + T_2(y+d, d, h) + 3k \qquad \text{if } y+d < h$$
$$T_2(y, d, h) = 0 \qquad \text{if } y+d \geqslant h$$

Hence:

$$T_2(y, d, h) = 3(k+1) + T_2(y+d, d, h) \qquad y+d < h$$
$$T_2(y+d, d, h) = 3k + T_2(y+2d), d, h) \qquad y+2d < h$$
$$\vdots$$
$$T_2(y+kd, d, h) = 3$$

Consequently,

$$T_2(y, d, h) = 3(1+2+\ldots+k+k+1) = \frac{3(k+1)(k+2)}{2}$$

5.6. Example 5 Traversing an acyclic graph

(Definitions of the graph-theoretic terms are given in Appendix 2.)

5.6.1. Algorithms

Consider a finite acyclic graph, in which the number of outgoing edges of each vertex is less than or equal to two (so there are at most two arcs attached to any one vertex). Each vertex is assigned a strictly positive integer weight. We assume that the graph is represented by records defined in the following way:

record *vertex* (**integer** *weight* ; **pointer**(*vertex*) *son*1,*son*2)

Example:

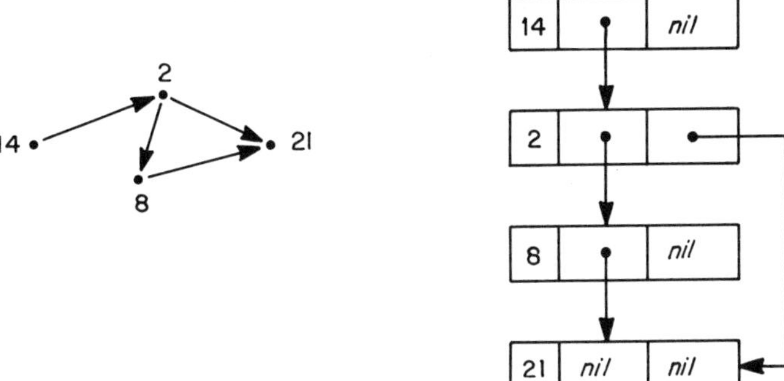

We wish to calculate the value $P(x)$, the maximum of the weights of the vertices which can be reached from vertex x.

5.6.1.1. The problem can be decomposed in the following way:

$$P(nil) = 0$$
$$P(x) = maximum\ (P(son1(x)), P(son2(x)), weight(x))$$

This immediately leads to the following procedure:

```
procedure maxweight1 ( pointer(vertex) value x ;
                       integer variable max ) ;
   if x = nil then max := 0
   else begin integer max1, max2 ;
         maxweight1 (son1(x),max1) ;
         maxweight1 (son2(x),max2) ;
         max := maximum (max1, max2, weight(x))
        end
```

The proof of partial correctness of this procedure is obvious.

Proof of termination
Let $A(x)$ be the set of vertices which can be reached from x. Suppose $A(x)$ has size $a(x)$.

For all x, we have $A(son1(x)) \subset A(x)$
and $A(son2(x)) \subset A(x)$.

These two inclusions are strict: indeed, we have $x \in A(x)$ and, as the graph is acylic, $x \notin A(son1(x))$ and $x \notin A(son2(x))$.

Let v be the function which for all w representing the values of the variables and parameters, gives $v(w) = a(x)$. The function v, with values in $\mathbb{N}$, is strictly decreasing along each path of the call tree of procedure *maxweight*1.

Analysis
Let n be the number of vertices in the graph. The execution time $T(x)$ of procedure *maxweight*1, for certain graphs, is an exponential function of n.

Example
Consider the following graph:

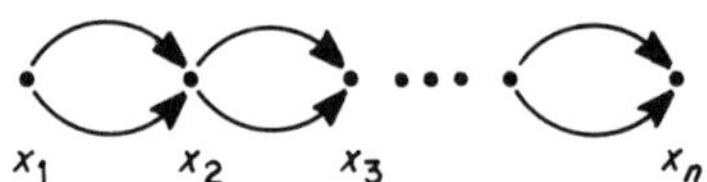

We have

$$T(x_i) = 2T(x_{i+1}) + C_1$$
$$T(nil) = C_2$$

Hence

$$T(x_1) = 2^n\,(C_1+C_2) - C_1$$

5.6.1.2. *Optimization*

The procedure we have just described corresponds to a traversal of all paths from origin x, which explains why its execution time can be exponential in n. Now, to solve the given problem, it is enough to consider each vertex which can be reached from x just once, independently of the actual paths. The decomposition described in the last section can lead to the execution of redundant computations: certain vertices which can be reached from $son1(x)$, and which were examined for the calculation of $P(son1(x))$, can also be reached from $son2(x)$, and taken into account once again for the calculation of $P(son2(x))$.

Let us reformulate the problem.

Let S by any set of vertices in the graph.

We define $R(S,x)$ to be the set of vertices y such that there exists a path from x to y which does not pass through a vertex of S. Let $P1(S,x)$ be the maximum of the weights of the vertices of $R(S,x)$. If $R(S,x) = \emptyset$, we can suppose $P1(S,x) = 0$. We thus have $P(x) = P1(\emptyset,x)$. Furthermore, the following relations hold:

$$R(S,x) = \emptyset \qquad \text{if } x = \text{nil or } x \in S$$
$$= R(S,son1(x)) \cup R(S,son2(x)) \cup \{x\} \qquad \text{otherwise.}$$

Hence the decomposition:

$$P1(S,x) = 0 \qquad \textit{if } x = \textit{nil} \text{ or } x \in S$$
$$= \textit{maximum}\ (\ P1(S,son1(x)),\ P1(S,son2(x)),\ weight(x)) \qquad \text{otherwise}$$

which is similar to the previous decomposition.

When the two sets $R(S,son1(x))$ and $R(S,son2(x))$ are not disjoint, the corresponding program will carry out redundant computations. The following property allows us to express $R(S,x)$ as the union of disjoint sets.

Property

$$R(S,x) \cup R(S,y) = R(S,x) \cup R(S \cup R(S,x), y)$$

Proof

The right-hand side of the equation is included in the left, as $R(S \cup T,y) \subset R(S,y)$ for all T.

The left-hand side is included in the right since, if $z \in R(S,y)$ and if $z \notin R(S \cup R(S,x),y)$, then $z \in R(S,x)$.

(Indeed, if $z \in R(S,y)$, there must exist a path from y to z which does not pass through a vertex of S. If $z \notin R(s \cup R(S,x), y)$, this path passes through a vertex of $S \cup R(S, x)$, and so through at least one vertex t of $R(S, x)$. We then have $t \in R(S,x)$ and $z \in R(S,t)$, and so $z \in R(S,x)$.)

Remark

This proof does not make use of the fact that the graph is acyclic. According to this property, if $x \neq nil$ and $x \notin S$, we have:

$$R(S,x) = R(S,son1(x)) \cup R(S \cup R(S,son1(x)),son2(x)) \cup \{x\}$$
$$= R(S,son2(x)) \cup R(S \cup R(S,son2(x)),son1(x)) \cup \{x\}$$

which leads to the equation:

$$\begin{aligned} P1(S,x) &= 0 \quad \text{if } x = nil \text{ or } x \in S \\ &\quad maximum\ (P1(S,son1(x)), \\ &\qquad P1(S \cup R(S,son1(x)),son2(x)), \\ &\qquad weight(x)) \quad \text{otherwise} \end{aligned}$$

It follows from this decomposition that the traversal which corresponds to the evaluation of $P1(\emptyset,x)$ avoids the redundant computations of *maxweight*1: each vertex of the graph which can be reached from x is only examined once.

On the other hand, in order to put this solution into practice, one must be able to evaluate the test '$x \in S$', at the point of each recursive call. A classic solution is to represent the characteristic function of the subset S by associating with each vertex of the graph a binary mark. To do this, an array of bits can be used. With the representation chosen in this section, it is simpler to put this information in the records. Hence, each vertex of the graph belonging to S carries a binary mark, and records are redefined in the following way:

record *vertex* (**integer** *weight* ; **pointer** (*vertex*) *son*1,*son*2 ;
Boolean *mark*)

The method for computing subset S is suggested by the fact that to calculate $P1(S,x)$, one must calculate both $P1(S, son1(x))$ and $P1(S \cup R(S, son1(x)), son2(x))$. Now the set $R(S, son1(x))$ is precisely the subset of vertices in the graph which we have to examine to calculate $P1(S, son1(x))$. Hence, to construct $S \cup R(S, son1(x))$, we simply have to add to S the vertices traversed during the computation of $P1(S, son1(x))$. The decomposition of $P1$ can therefore be used directly to describe the algorithm for marking the vertices of S. We shall therefore write a recursive procedure which computes $P(S,x)$ and, at the same time, marks the vertices being examined. We first put in a recursive call to compute $P1(S, son1(x))$ and, simultaneously, to mark the vertices of $R(S, son1(x))$. At the end of this call, the set of marked vertices is $S \cup R(S, son1(x))$. After the second recursive call, the set of marked vertices is $S \cup R(S, son1(x)) \cup R(S, son2(x))$. And for the procedure to be correct, we still have to mark vertex x itself. We therefore have the following procedure:

```
procedure maxweight2 (pointer(vertex) value x ; integer variable max);
if (x = nil) oriffalse mark(x) then max := 0
else
   begin integer max1, max2 ;
      maxweight2(son1(x),max1) ;
      maxweight2(son2(x),max2) ;
      max := maximum(max1,max2,weight(x)) ;
      mark(x) := true
   end
```

It is of course necessary to suppose that, for the principal call, no vertex of the graph is marked, since $P(x) = P1(\emptyset,x)$.

Exercise
Calculate, as a function of n, the number of vertices in the graph which can be reached from x and the number of recursive calls invoked by the principal call *maxweight2(x,max)*.
Calculate the execution time of procedure *maxweight2*.

5.6.2. Application—Eliminating redundant computations in a recursive program

The following procedure calculates C_n^p according to the decomposition given in section 5.1.4.

```
procedure combination1 (integer value n,p ; integer variable r) ;
if p = 0 or p = n then r := 1
else
   begin integer r1, r2 ;
      combination1 (n−1,p,r1) ;
      combination1 (n−1, p−1, r2) ;
      r := r1 + r2
   end
```

Procedure *combination1* is similar to procedure *maxweight1* of the preceding section. The actual computations, for inputs n and p, correspond to the traversal of the following (acyclic) graph:

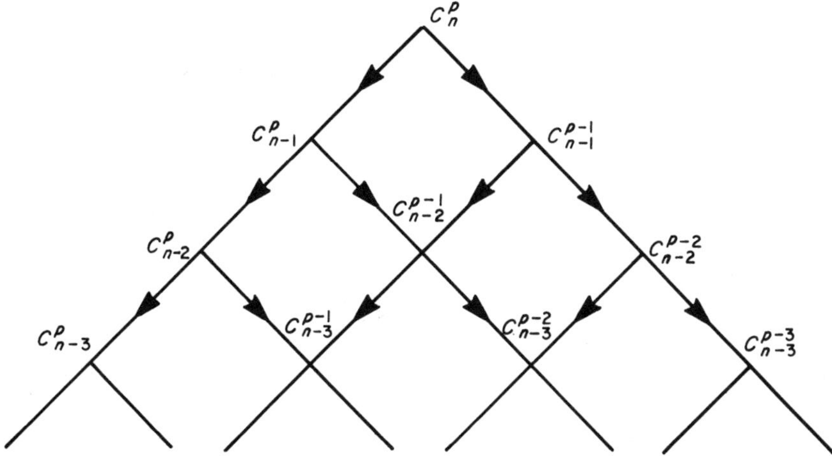

This graph is derived from the call tree of the procedure by identifying the vertices labelled with recursive calls which calculate the same C_i^j. Procedure *combination*1 is inefficient, for the same reason that procedure *maxweight*1 is: it corresponds to a traversal without marking and consequently entails redundant computations.

The method which allowed us to obtain *maxweight*2 can be applied to this problem. It involves associating a mark with each vertex of the graph. As the graph is only implicit—with a vertex characterized by the pair (n,p)—we shall use a logical array, called *mark*. But a traversal with marking only calculates C_n^p if we keep the results associated with the vertices already traversed. For this we shall use an array of integers, called c.

```
procedure combination2 (integer value n,p ; integer variable r) ;
if p = 0 or p = n then r := 1
else if mark(n,p) then r := c(n,p)
   else
      begin integer r1, r2 ;
         combination2 (n-1,p,r1) ;
         combination2 (n-1,p-1,r2) ;
         r := r1 + r2 ;
         mark(n,p) := true ;
         c(n,p) := r
      end
```

Optimization
Marking is a way of identifying vertices already encountered in order to avoid redundant computations. However, we have seen in section 5.5 an example

where it is possible to eliminate redundant operations without using markers. Procedure *triangles*1 corresponds to the traversal of the following graph (which is similar to the one used for calculating C_n^p).

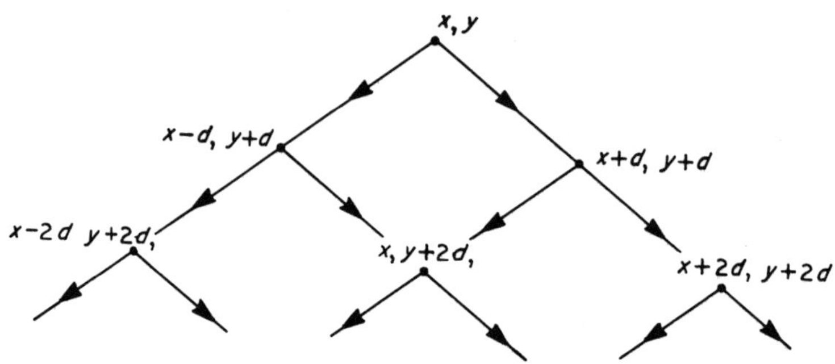

The derivation of procedure *triangles*2 consisted in defining a traversal of vertices using the following sub-graph:

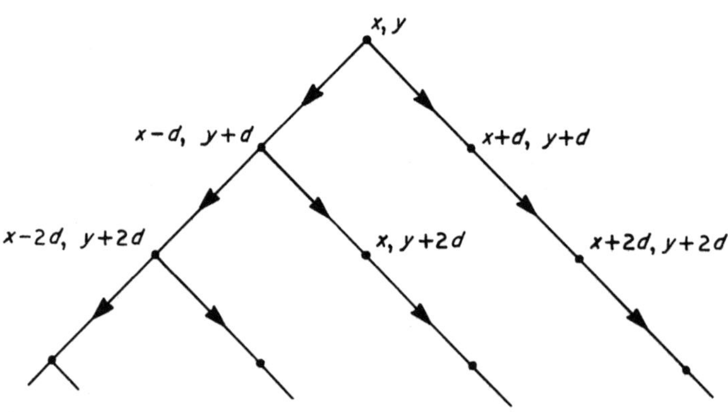

In a similar vein, we can define a calculation of C_n^p which avoids redundant computations without making use of markers.

```
procedure combi1 (integer value n, p ; integer variable r) ;
if p = 0 or p = n then r := 1
else
   begin integer r1, r2 ;
      combi1 (n−1,p,r1) ;
      combi2 (n−1,p−1, r2) ;
      r := r1 + r2 ;
      c(n,p) := r
   end

procedure combi2 (integer value n, p ; integer variable r) ;
if p = 0 or p = n then r := 1
else
   begin integer r1, r2 ;
      r1 := if n−1 = p then 1 else c(n−1,p) ;
      combi2 (n−1,p−1,r2) ;
      r := r1 + r2 ;
      c(n,p) := r
   end
```

The call tree associated with the principal call *combi*1(n, p, r) has the following form.

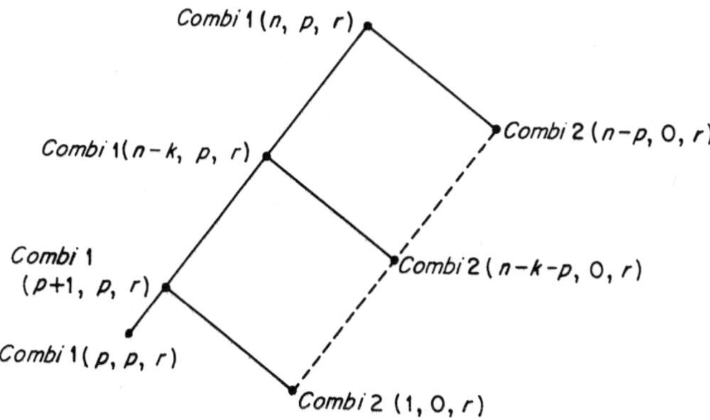

We note that:

At a call of procedure *combi*2, the condition $p = n$ will always be false. At a recursive call of procedure *combi*1, the condition $p=0$ will always be false: nevertheless, we retain the corresponding test for principal calls of the form *combi*1(n, 0, r).
The values of C_n^p calculated by a call of *combi*1 are not reused by a later computation, so there is no point in saving them.
It is not necessary to use a two-dimensional array to keep the values of C_n^p calculated by a call of *combi*2, since only the last p values calculated are needed, and no value is used more than once.

We can therefore derive the following procedures:

```
procedure combi1 (integer value n, p ; integer variable r) ;
if p = 0 or p = n then r := 1
else
   begin integer r1, r2 ;
      combi1 (n-1,p,r1) ;
      combi2 (n-1,p-1,r2) ;
      r := r1 + r2
   end

procedure combi2 (integer value n,p ; integer variable r) ;
if p = 0 then r := 1
else
   begin integer r1, r2 ;
      r1 := if n-1 = p then 1 else c(p) ;
      combi2 (n-1,p-1,r2) ;
      r := r1 + r2 ;
      c(p) := r
   end
```

Exercises

(1) Calculate the number of additions carried out by procedures *combination*1 and *combination*2 for calculating C_n^p.

(2) The sequence of Fibonacci numbers is defined by:

$f_0 = f_1 = 1$

$f_n = f_{n-1} + f_{n-2} \quad \text{for } n > 1.$

Construct a program for calculating f_n based on this recursive definition. Analyse this program. Construct an optimized program for calculating f_n, such that f_i for $i \leqslant n$ is calculated once only. Analyse this program and compare it with the preceding one.

5.6.3. Topological sort

Let us return to the problem posed in section 5.6.1.

To calculate the maximum weight $P(x)$, we must first calculate the values of $P(son1(x))$ and $P(son2(x))$. The value of $P(x)$ for different vertices x cannot be calculated in any order. More precisely, if there exists a path of length $\geqslant 1$, from x to y, $P(y)$ must be calculated before $P(x)$. This defines a partial ordering on the vertices of the graph. The order in which the procedure *maxweight*2 calculates $P(x)$ is a total ordering compatible with this partial ordering.

Definitions

Given an acyclic graph G, we define the following partial ordering on the set of vertices of G:

$x \leqslant y$ if and only if there exists a path from x to y.

Any total order compatible with this relation is called a *topological order*.

We call the calculation of a topological order of the vertices of G the *topological sort* of the vertices of G.

The procedure *maxweight*2 computes $P(y)$, for each vertex y of the graph reachable from x, once and only once, by following a topological order.

A procedure *topsort* for obtaining a topological sort can easily be derived from this procedure.

Suppose the graph is represented by records of two kinds:

record *vertex* (**pointer**(*arc*) *successor*1 ; **Boolean** *mark*)
record *arc* (**pointer**(*vertex*) *target* ; **pointer**(*arc*) *next*)

The following procedure constructs a sequence S of vertices in the graph. If we take $(s_1, s_2, \ldots, s_k)$ to be the value of S, then after execution of *insert*(x), the value of S will be $(x, s_1, s_2, \ldots, s_k)$.

```
procedure topsort (pointer(vertex) value x) ;
if ¬ mark(x) then
begin pointer(arc) y ;
   y := successor1 (x) ;
   while y ≠ nil do
   begin
      topsort (target(y)) ;
      y := next(y)
   end
   insert(x) ;
   mark(x) := true
end
```

A call of *topsort*(x), with sequence S empty and no vertex marked, will produce the sequence of all vertices which can be reached from x, arranged in topological order.

If, according to the partial ordering previously defined, the set of vertices in the graph includes only one minimal element r (that is, only one vertex without a predecessor), the principal call *topsort*(r) constructs a topological order of the vertices in this graph. If more than one vertex in the graph has no predecessor, the procedure calls for each of these vertices are invoked in turn. For a principal call *topsort*(r), occurring when the vertices added to S by previous calls have been marked, we add to S the collection of vertices which can be reached from r, and which have not already been encountered. Such a sequence of principal calls constructs a topological order of vertices in the graph.

Application
Consider an acyclic graph G such that:
— each vertex represents a task;
— an arc leading from x to y means that execution of task x cannot begin before completion of task y.
A topological sort of the vertices in the graph defines an order in which the tasks can be executed: it is sufficient to traverse S, the sequence obtained, in reverse order.

Exercise
Suppose each task has an associated execution time. Tasks can be executed simultaneously (provided the constraints on the sequence of arcs in the graph are respected).

Modify the procedure *topsort* to calculate the minimum time necessary for executing all the tasks.

Comments and Bibliography

Recursive programming is important because it is easy: when the function to be calculated is defined recursively, the recursive program is very close to its definition, and the construction and proof of the program is thereby greatly simplified.

The essential problem is choosing a recursive definition which will lead to an efficient program. In this chapter, two fundamental principles have been stated: first, one tries to decompose the problem into sub-problems of equal size and, second, one tries to avoid redundant computations. We have shown with the examples in sections 5.5 and 5.6 how to get from a recursive definition which is simple but inefficient, to a more complicated recursive definition which produces an efficient program. The given rules can also be applied directly to the original program, so they can be considered as transformation rules for recursive programs. For more details, the reader can refer to the articles by Burstall and Darlington (1977) and Bird (1980). Sorting by partitioning (quicksort) is due to Hoare. A fuller analysis can be found in the article by Sedgewick (1977).

Chapter 6

Elimination of Recursion

6.1. Introduction

In the preceding chapters, we have studied *iterative programs*, which are constructed from primitive instructions with tests, loops, and non-recursive procedures, and *recursive programs*, which also allow recursive procedures. The latter class is an extension of the former, although it does not allow us to compute any more functions, since a recursive program can always be translated into an equivalent iterative one.

It follows that, whatever the problem to be solved, we can choose to construct either a recursive or an iterative program. If the problem lends itself naturally to a recursive decomposition, the recursive program can simply reproduce the chosen decomposition, and is consequently clearer and easier to prove than an equivalent iterative program. This is the case, for example, for sorting by partitioning, the drawing programs and the algorithms for traversing graphs seen in the last chapter.

Recursive programming nevertheless has its disadvantages:

Certain programming languages (FORTRAN, COBOL, and machine languages, for instance) do not permit recursion.

It is often costly, in terms of the execution time and storage space required.

These disadvantages can be minimized by transforming a given recursive program into an iterative program. The method of program transformation will be illustrated in this chapter by a number of examples: sorting by partitioning, the towers of Hanoi problem and the Schorr and Waite algorithm. Such a method is more efficient than directly constructing an iterative program, especially when this turns out to be complicated and therefore difficult to prove correct. Indeed, if the recursive program has been proved correct, and if the transformations preserve correctness, then the iterative program thus obtained is guaranteed to be correct, without a direct proof being required.

There are different ways of transforming recursive programs into iterative programs. For example, every compiler for a programming language which allows recursive procedures must translate recursive programs into iterative ones, since machine languages do not allow recursion. The transformations used in this situation are similar to those studied in section 6.3.

At the end of this chapter, we shall present an example of transformation in which the computations carried out by the recursive program are optimized: those associated with redundant recursive calls are deleted.

Finally, we shall restrict attention to *simple* recursions. Adaptation to mutual recursions is not difficult and will be left as an exercise.

6.2. Elimination of tail recursion

6.2.1. Definition

If, in the body of a procedure, a recursive call is placed in such a way that its execution is *never* followed by the execution of another instruction of the procedure, this call is known as a *tail recursive call*.

The execution of such a call terminates the execution of the body of the procedure.

Examples

(1) The two recursive calls of the binary search procedure (§5.3.1).
(2) The first recursive call of procedure *m* (§4.4.1).
(3) The second recursive call of sorting by partitioning (§5.4.1).

Explanation of terminology. In every execution tree, a vertex associated with a tail recursive call is always a vertex 'at the rightmost point of the tree'. The term 'tail' thus refers to the order in which instructions *are executed* and not necessarily to the order in which they appear in the *text* of the procedure.

Examples

Consider a procedure *p* of the form:

procedure *p* ; **if** *A* **then begin** *B* ; *p* **end else** *C*

Here, the recursive call of *p* is a tail recursion. A corresponding execution tree might be:

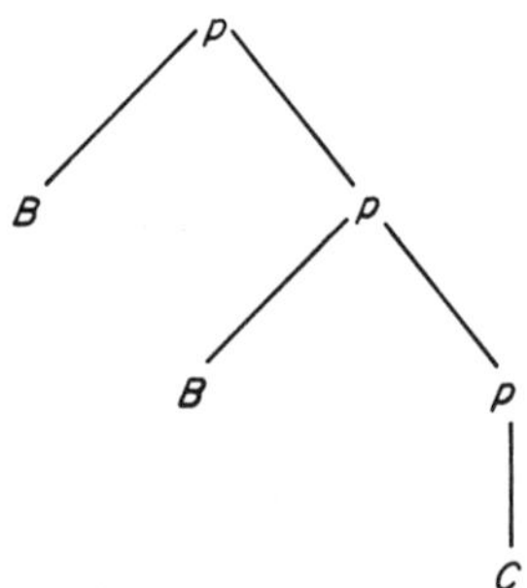

Consider a procedure q of the form:

procedure q ; **while** A **do begin** B ; q **end**

In this case, the recursive call is not a tail recursion. A corresponding execution tree might be as shown below.

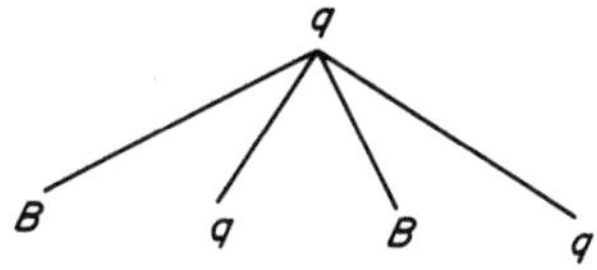

6.2.2. Method

A procedure p which includes a tail recursive call can be represented as follows:

procedure p (**variable** $\overline{x}$; **value** $\overline{y}$) :

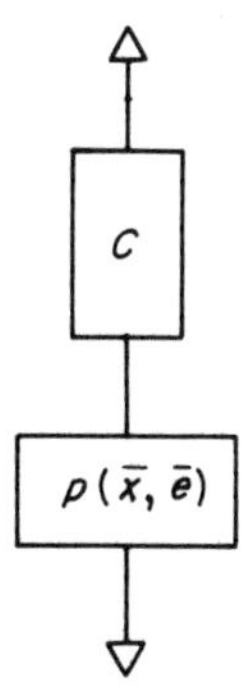

where

$\overline{x}$ and $\overline{y}$ are the lists of formal variable and formal value parameters.

$p(\overline{x},\overline{e})$ is the tail recursive call being considered, and $\overline{e}$ the list of actual value parameters of this call. For the actual variable parameters, we consider only the case where these are the same as the formal variable parameters $\overline{x}$.

C is the flowchart of the body of procedure p, apart from the recursive call being considered.

The symbol Δ comes before execution of the first instruction.

The symbol ∇ marks the end of execution. If such a symbol does not appear in C, then procedure p loops.

The method for eliminating tail recursion derives from the following lemma, which we give without proof:

Lemma
Procedure p defined by:

procedure p (**variable** $\bar{x}$; **value** $\bar{y}$) :

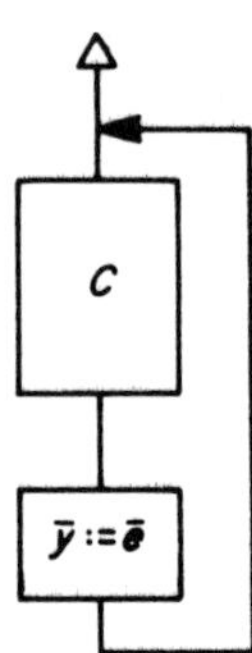

is equivalent to procedure p defined by:

procedure p (**variable** $\bar{x}$; **value** $\bar{y}$) :

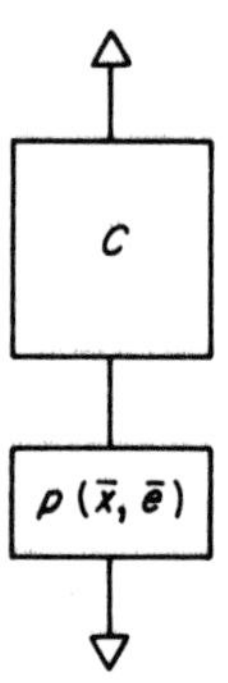

6.2.3. Examples

6.2.3.1. *Sorting by partitioning* (see §5.4)

Using the above lemma, we obtain the following procedure:

```
procedure sort (integer value inf, sup) ;
   while inf < sup do
   begin integer i ;
         partition(i) ;
         sort (inf, i−1) ;
         inf := i+1
   end
```

which would be better written:

```
procedure sort (integer value inf, sup) ;
begin integer i ;
   while inf < sup do
   begin
      partition(i) ;
      sort (inf, i-1) ;
      inf := i+1
   end
end
```

6.2.3.2. *Multiplication procedure* (see §4.1)

We obtain the following procedure:

```
procedure m (integer value x, y ; integer variable r) ;
BEG : if y=0 then r:=0
        else if even(y) then
                begin x:=x*2 ; y:=y div 2 ; goto BEG end
                else
                begin m(x*2, y div 2, r) ; r:=r+x end
```

which can be rewritten more elegantly as:

```
procedure m (integer value x, y ; integer variable r) ;
   begin
      while y=0 and even (y) do
         begin x:=x*2 ; y:=y div 2 end ;
      if y=0 then r:=0
      else begin m (x*2, y div 2, r) ; r:=r+x end
   end
```

6.2.3.3. *Exercise*

Eliminate the two tail recursions from the binary search procedure of section 5.3.1.

6.2.4. Conclusion

Elimination of tail recursion is simple and shortens execution time quite considerably. We have registered gains of 20 to 25 per cent for the two examples in the last section (in PL/1, Multics system, as well as in ALGOLW, with an IBM/360). This type of elimination is therefore definitely interesting in its own right. It is not, however, a necessary stage in the elimination of all recursive calls. In particular, compilers do not normally deal with the case of tail recursions separately, and this explains the gain in time mentioned above.

6.3. Elimination of recursion in the general case

The complete elimination of recursion takes place in two stages:

(a) Elimination of local parameters and variables;
(b) Transformation of a recursive procedure with no local parameters or variables into an equivalent iterative procedure.

6.3.1. Elimination of local parameters and variables

In this section, variables declared in the same block as the procedure will be called *global* variables.

6.3.1.1. *Elimination of variable parameters*

We shall consider only the case where:

the actual parameters of recursive calls are the same as the corresponding formal parameters;
the actual parameters of the principal call can be accessed from anywhere in the body of the procedure.

For each occurrence of a formal variable parameter, we can then substitute the corresponding actual parameter of the principal call.

6.3.1.2. *Elimination of value parameters*

We eliminate value parameters (and local variables):

by saving their values with the help of a stack, and then replacing them with global variables.

A stack is a sequence of values, manipulated with the help of the three primitives, *push*, *pop*, and *emptystack*, defined in section 3.3.4.

Remarks

(i) The sequence: $push(x);pop(x)$
is equivalent to the empty instruction.
Is this the case with the sequence: $pop(x);push(x)$?

(ii) For the sake of simplicity, we shall write:
$push\ (expr_1,expr_2, \ldots)$
instead of $push(expr_1);push(expr_2); \ldots$
and $pop(x_1,x_2, \ldots)$
instead of $pop(x_1);pop(x_2); \ldots$

(iii) Given the instruction *push*($\bar{y}$), where $\bar{y}$ is a list of variables, the inverse operation will be executed by *pop*($\tilde{\bar{y}}$), where the list $\tilde{\bar{y}}$ is the mirror-image of $\bar{y}$. For instance, the sequence *push*(y_1, y_2, y_3);*pop*(y_3, y_2, y_1) is equivalent to the empty instruction.

Let *p* be a recursive procedure of the form:

procedure *p* (**value** $\bar{y}$).

We obtain a procedure equivalent to *p* by replacing each recursive call *p*($\bar{e}$) by the sequence:

push($\bar{y}$) ; $\bar{y}$:= $\bar{e}$; *p*($\bar{y}$) ; *pop*($\tilde{\bar{y}}$)

We can then write *p* in the form of a procedure without parameters, manipulating global variables, according to the following definition:

variable $\overline{yg}$;
procedure *p* ; body of *p*

where

yg_i are global variables which replace the value parameters y_i;
the new body of procedure *p* is obtained
by substituting for each occurrence of a value parameter y_i the corresponding global variable yg_i, and by replacing each recursive call *p*($\bar{y}$) by the recursive call *p*.

A principal call of *p*, *p*($\bar{u}$), is replaced by the sequence

$\overline{yg}$:= $\bar{u}$; *p*

6.3.1.3. *Elimination of local variables*

The transformation of local variables into global variables is achieved in the same way as that of value parameters. A value parameter may in fact be considered as an initialized local variable. So, if *vg* is a global variable which replaces a local variable *v*, the value of *vg* will be pushed before, and popped after, each recursive call.

Remark

To define the evaluation of a recursive procedure (§4.1.3), we introduced the idea of 'uninitialized' variables. The stack used here is a device which allows us to represent and minimize the number of these variables. We implicitly adopted such a structure to define the amount of storage space required to execute a procedure call (§4.5.2).

6.3.1.4. *Example*

Consider the sorting by partitioning procedure containing two recursive calls (§5.4). This procedure has two value parameters, *inf* and *sup*, and a local variable, *i*. We obtain the following program:

```
integer infg, supg, ig ;
procedure sort ;
if infg < supg then
begin
    partition (infg, supg, ig) ;
    push (infg, supg, ig) ; supg := ig − 1 ;
    sort ;
    pop (ig, supg, infg) ;
    push (infg, supg, ig) ; infg := ig+1 ;
    sort ;
    pop (ig, supg, infg)
end
```

6.3.1.5. *Optimizations*

Using a stack to save the value of each value parameter and each local parameter is a systematic method found in compilers. It can often be improved upon when the particular properties of the transformed program are taken into account.

6.3.1.5.1. *Use of inverse functions* Consider a recursive procedure of the form **procedure** p(**value** $\bar{y}$) and let $p(\bar{e})$ be a recursive call.

As we have seen, the call $p(\bar{e})$ is replaced by the sequence A:

$push(\overline{yg}, \overline{vg})$; $\overline{yg} := \bar{e}$; p ; $pop(\widetilde{\overline{vg}}, \widetilde{\overline{yg}})$

where $\overline{yg}$ and $\overline{vg}$ are global variables which replace, respectively, the value parameters and local parameters of p.

The sequence $\overline{yg} := \bar{e}$; p in general can modify the values of $\overline{yg}$ and $\overline{vg}$. The instruction $pop(\widetilde{\overline{vg}}, \widetilde{\overline{yg}})$ restores the previous values of these variables. So we have:

$(\overline{yg} = \overline{yg_0})$ & $(\overline{vg} = \overline{vg_0})$
$\{A\}$
$(\overline{yg} = \overline{yg_0})$ & $(\overline{v_g} = \overline{vg_0})$

If we can find a sequence of instructions B which calculates the values $\overline{yg_0}$ and $\overline{vg_0}$ after execution of the recursive call p, we will have:

$(\overline{yg} = \overline{yg_0})$ & $(\overline{vg} = \overline{vg_0})$
$\{\overline{yg} := \bar{e}\ ;\ p\ ;\ B\}$
$(\overline{yg} = \overline{yg_0})$ & $(\overline{vg} = \overline{vg_0})$

In such a case, there is no point in using a stack. Note that we had to deal with a similar problem in section 2.4.1. The difficulty, of course, is finding such a sequence B and proving it correct.

Let X_B be the set of program variables whose values are used in sequence B. If the recursive call p does not modify the values of the variables of X_B, then sequence B will be easier to write and to prove. In the simplest cases, it computes the *inverse function* of $f_{\overline{yg}:=\bar{e}}$ (see example 2 below). By an abuse of language, we shall use this term each time a sequence of instructions is employed to restore the initial values of $\overline{yg}$ and $\overline{vg}$.

Remarks

(i) It is possible in certain cases that only the values of certain yg_i or vg_i can be recalculated. We then combine the two methods, using a stack for the other variables.

(ii) If, for a certain i, we have $yg_i{=}e_i$, and if p does not modify yg_i, it is obviously pointless to save this variable. The functions $f_{yg_i:=e_i}$ and $f^{-1}_{yg_i:=e_i}$ are then both the identity function (see example 3 below).

Example 1

Consider the following procedure:

```
procedure p (integer value x) ;
begin
   x:=x−1 ; y:=y∗x ;
   if x≥0 then begin p(x−1) ; y:=y+x end
end
```

This is equivalent to:

```
integer x ;
procedure p ;
begin
   x:=x−1 ; y:=y∗x ;
   if x≥0 then begin x:=x−1 ; p ; x:=x+2 ; y:=y+x end
end
```

One can verify, as an exercise, that

$(x{=}x_0)\ \{p\}\ (x{=}x_0{-}1)$

From this it follows that

$(x{=}x_0)\ \{x{:=}x{-}1\ ;\ p\ ;\ x{:=}x{+}2\}\ (x{=}x_0)$

Example 2

Consider the following procedure:

```
procedure p (integer value x) ;
begin
   y:=y∗x ;
   if x≥0 then begin p(x−1) ; y:=y+x end
end
```

This is equivalent to:

```
integer x ;
procedure p ;
begin
   y:=y*x ;
   if x≥0 then begin x:=x−1 ; p ; x:=x+1 ; y:=y+x end
end
```

One can verify, as an exercise, that

$(x=x_0)$ $\{p\}$ $(x=x_0)$

and so

$(x=x_0)$ $\{x{:=}x-1 \; ; \; p \; ; \; x{:=}x+1\}$ $(x=x_0)$

Here, the recursive call p does not modify the value of x, and the instruction $x{:=}x+1$ computes the inverse function of $f_{x:=x-1}$.

Example 3

Consider the following procedure:

```
procedure p (integer value x,z) ;
begin
   y := y*x ;
   if x≥z then begin p(x−1, z) ; y:=y+x end
end
```

This is equivalent to:

```
integer x ;
procedure p ;
begin
   y:=y*x ;
   if x≥z then begin x:=x−1 ; p ; x:=x+1 ; y:=y+x end
end
```

One can verify that

$(z=z_0)$ $\{p\}$ $(z=z_0)$

Hence

$(z=z_0)$ $\{z{:=}z \; ; \; p \; ; \; z{:=}z\}$ $(z=z_0)$

Here, the two assignments $z{:=}z$, which compute the identity function, obviously do not appear in the final form of the procedure.

6.3.1.5.2. Clearly, there is no point in saving the value of a local parameter or variable before a recursive call if this value is not going to be used after the call.

In particular, this is the case for *every tail recursive call*.

Example
Consider the procedure:

```
procedure p (integer value x) ;
begin
   y:=y*x ;
   if x>0 then begin p(x div 2) ; y:=y+1 end
end
```

This is equivalent to:

```
integer x ;
procedure p ;
begin
   y:=y*x ;
   if x>0 then begin x:=x div 2 ; p ; y:=y+1 end
end
```

Remark
In contrast to what we saw in the last section, the statement $(x=x_0)$ $\{p\}$ $(x=x_0)$ is in general false. The value of the global variable is not preserved.

6.3.1.5.3. *Application. Sorting by partitioning.* The program given in §6.3.1.4 can be improved in various ways. These are described in the following table:

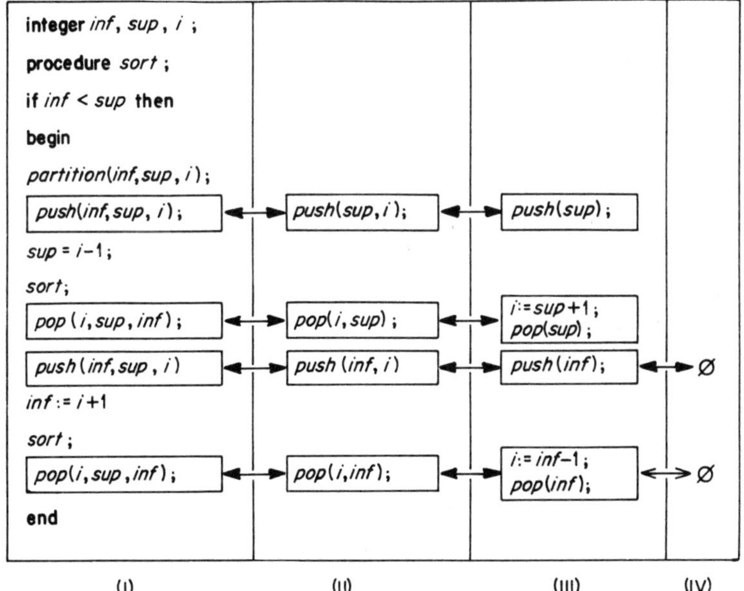

(I) is the program in §6.3.1.4.

(II) is based on the observation that *inf* is not modified by the first recursive call and that *sup* is not modified by the second (the inverse function is the identity function).

(III) is obtained by using inverse functions to restore the value of *i* after the first and second call.

We can pass from (III) to (IV) by observing that there is no point in preserving *i*, and therefore *inf*, for the second call, since their values are not used afterwards.

The final program (IV) is therefore:

```
integer inf, sup, i ;
procedure sort ;
if inf < sup then
begin
   partition (inf,sup,i) ;
   push (sup) ;
   sup := i−1 ;
   sort ;
   inf := sup+2 ;
   pop (sup) ;
   sort
end
```

We can verify that this program is correct by proving the following lemma by induction: 'program (IV) preserves *sup*, and is correct'.

Remarks

(i) The second recursive call of this procedure is a tail recursive call. If we eliminate it, we discover a program which can also be obtained by transforming the procedure in §6.2.3.1 into a procedure without parameters. But this is not always the case: the elimination of tail recursion can make it impossible for certain inverse functions to be used, given that the values of certain variables are no longer preserved (on this point, see the remark in section 6.3.1.5.2, the towers of Hanoi, §6.4.1, and the Schorr and Waite algorithm, §6.4.2.4).

(ii) We have replaced the sequence:

i:=*sup*+1 ; *pop* (*sup*) ; *inf*:=*i*+1

by its equivalent:

inf:=*sup*+2 ; *pop* (*sup*).

6.3.2. Elimination of recursion

Having used the results described in the last section, we can return to the problem of eliminating recursion in a procedure which has no local parameters or variables.

6.3.2.1. *Procedures with only one recursive call*

A procedure with only one recursive call can be represented in the following way:

procedure p :

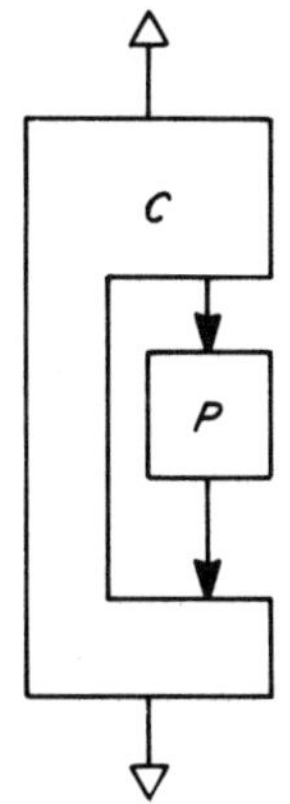

where

C is the flowchart of the body of the procedure, apart from the recursive call;

the symbol Δ precedes the first instruction executed;

the symbol ∇ marks the end of execution (it does not appear in C).

This procedure is equivalent to the following one:

procedure p :

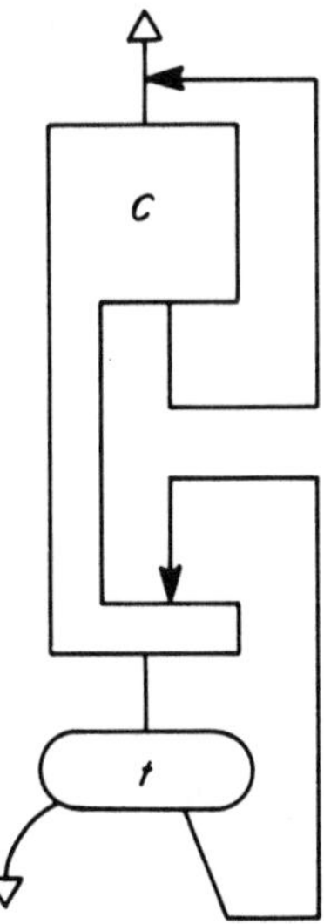

where

C is unchanged;

the recursive call is replaced by a jump to the first instruction of C to be executed;

the symbol ∇ is replaced by a test t, used to distinguish between two cases: the end of the principal call, when execution is finished, or, the end of a recursive call, when a jump is made to the instruction of C executed immediately after the recursive call.

A systematic method for programming test t consists in using a counter, represented for instance by an integer variable, as shown in the diagram below.

procedure p :

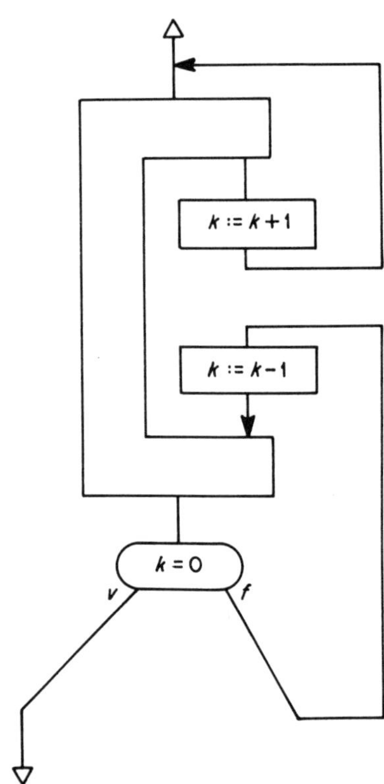

Examples:

(1) Consider a procedure of the form:

procedure p ; **if** *cond* **then begin** A ; p B **end else** C

The flowchart of (recursive procedure) p:

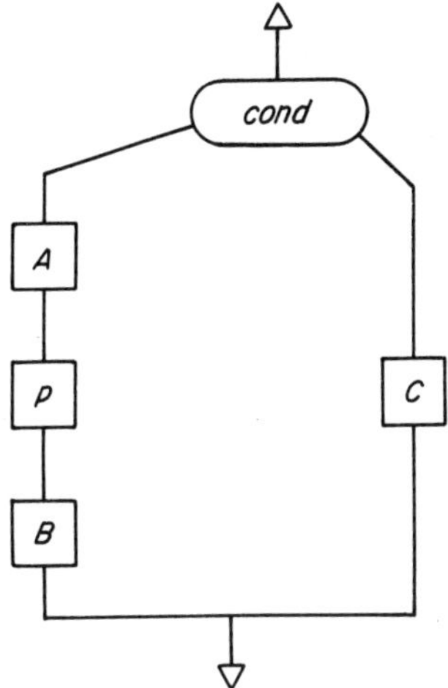

becomes (iterative procedure):

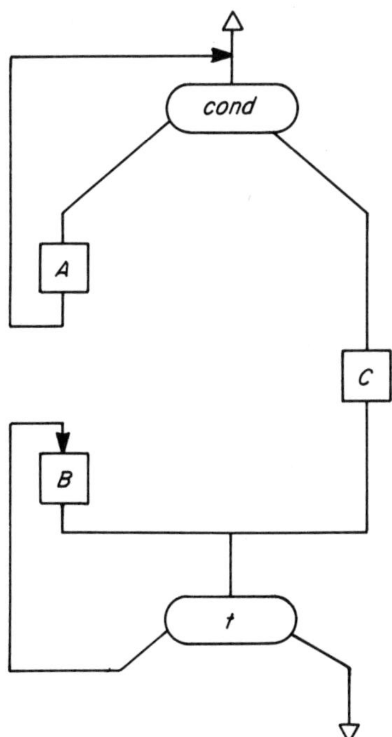

Supposing that A, B, and C do not contain a reference to a variable k, the transformation leads to the following procedure:

```
procedure p ;
begin integer k ;
   k := 0 ;
   while cond do begin A ; k := k+1 end ;
   C ;
   while k ≠ 0 do begin k := k−1 ; B end
end
```

(2) Consider a procedure of the form:

```
procedure p ; while cond do begin A ; p ; B end
```

The flowchart of (recursive procedure) p:

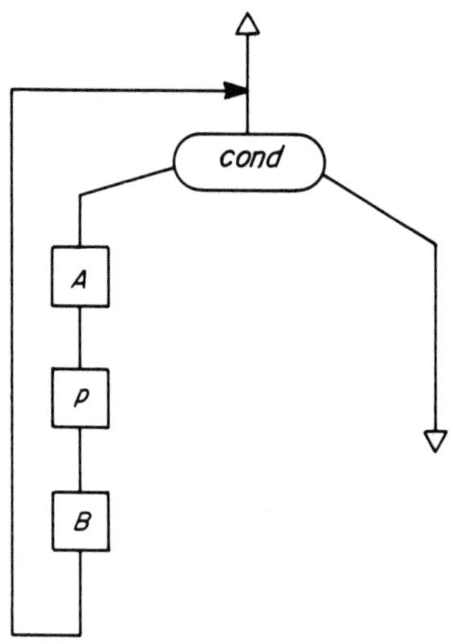

becomes (iterative procedure): (see top, opposite)

Supposing that A and B do not include a reference to a variable k, the transformation leads to the following procedure:

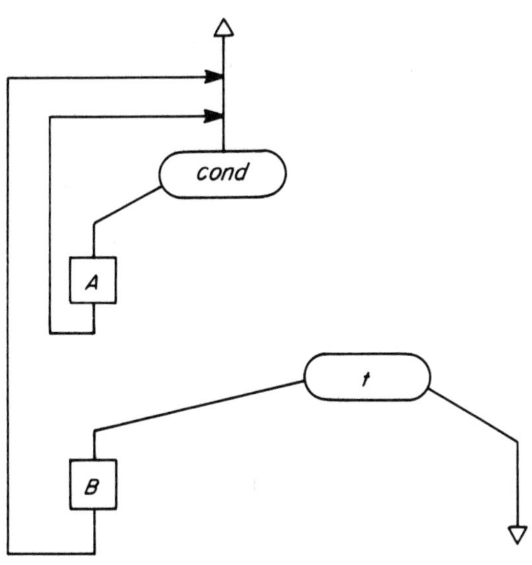


```
procedure p ;
begin integer k ;
   k := 0 ;
BEG : while cond do begin A ; k := k+1 end ;
   if k ≠ 0 then begin k := k−1 ; B goto BEG end
end
```

Remark

It is often possible to define test *t* with the help of the values of the program variables, or the value on top of the stack (used to eliminate local parameters and variables), without introducing any additional variables.

Application. Sorting by partitioning

Program (IV), obtained in §6.3.1.5.3, becomes after elimination of the tail recursive call :

```
integer inf, sup, i ;
procedure sort ;
while inf < sup do
begin
   partition (inf,sup,i) ;
   push (sup) ;
   sup := i−1 ;
   sort ;
   inf := sup+2 ;
   pop (sup)
end
```

Procedure *sort* is the same as in example (2) in the last section. There is, however, no point in introducing an additional variable *k*. Supposing the stack is initially empty, the program becomes:

```
integer inf, sup i ;
procedure sort ;
begin
   BEG : while inf < sup do
            begin partition(inf,sup,i) ; push(sup) ; sup:=i−1 end ;
            if ¬ emptystack then
            begin inf:=sup+2 ; pop(sup) ; goto BEG end
end
```

This program is similar to the one generated by a compiler for procedure *sort* in section 6.2.3.1. The major improvement concerns the size of the stack: for each recursive call, only *sup* is stacked, instead of *inf*, *sup*, *i*, and the return address.

6.3.2.2. *Procedure with several recursive calls*

The transformation described in the last section can easily be generalized to the case of several recursive calls.

(a) Each recursive call will, as before, be replaced by a jump to the beginning of the body of the procedure.
(b) Test *t* is now insufficient by itself. It has to be replaced by a sequence of tests t_1, t_2, . . . , in order to distinguish between the different recursive calls, as well as the principal call.

These tests can be carried out with the help of a stack, which corresponds to the idea of the return address stack used by compilers. For instance, value *k* is stacked before the corresponding jump to the *k*th recursive call; in order to carry out the tests, the stack is popped. The empty stack corresponds to the end of the principal call.

This stack, whose alphabet is finite, can be the same as the stack of values of local parameters and variables. It can also be programmed with an integer variable: the counter mentioned in the last section represents a stack with an alphabet of only one symbol; in the case of a procedure which includes *n* recursive calls, the integer variable is manipulated by modulo *n* operations (see §6.4.1).

As before, it is often possible to define the tests t_1, t_2, . . . by using only the given program variables and the top of the stack.

Example
Consider a procedure of the form:

```
procedure p ; if cond then begin A ; p ; B ; p ; C end else D
```

The flowchart of (recursive procedure) *p*:

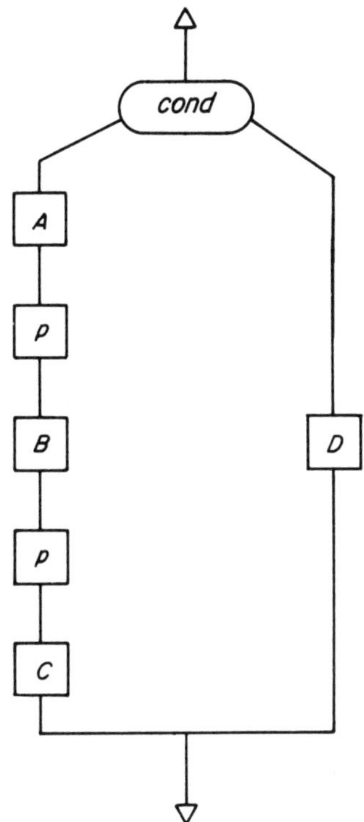

becomes (iterative procedure): (p. 126)

Supposing the stack is initially empty, and that *A*, *B*, *C*, and *D* do not refer to a variable *i*, the transformation of this procedure leads to:

```
procedure p ;
begin integer i ;
BEG :   while cond do begin A ; push(1) end ;
        D ;
EXIT :  if ¬ emptystack then
        begin pop(i);
           if i=1 then begin B ; push(2) ; goto BEG end
           else begin C ; goto EXIT end
        end
end
```

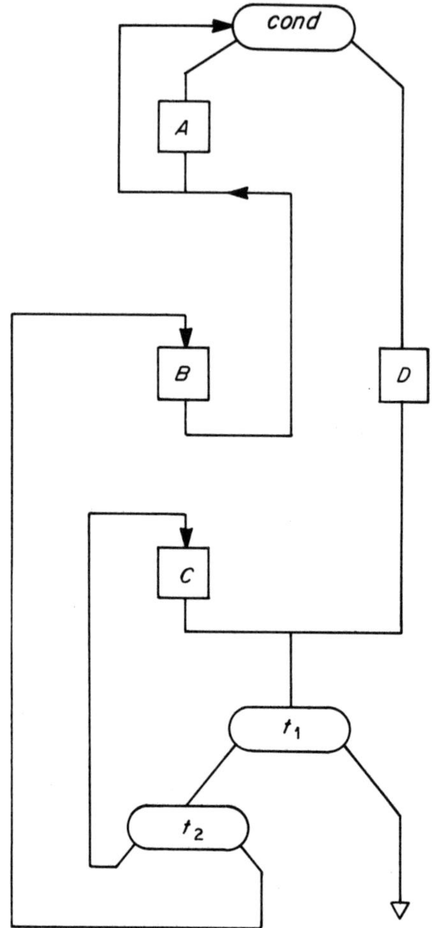

In this iterative procedure, the first while loop produces sequences of executions of A corresponding to the initial parts of the executions of the recursive procedure.

In the same way, the second loop produces sequences of executions of C corresponding to the final parts. Let us look at this second loop.

Consider the primitive *topofstack*, whose value is the value at the top of the stack (the stack is not modified). The primitive *pop*, which has no parameter, removes the value at the top of the stack (provided the stack is not empty).

The procedure just described can then be written:

```
procedure p ;
begin
BEG : while cond do begin A ; push(1) end ;
      D ;
      while (¬ emptystack andiftrue topofstack=2) do
      begin pop ; C end ;
      if ¬ emptystack then
      begin pop ; B ; push(2) ; goto BEG end
end
```

We may also choose to represent the stack by an integer variable k, initialized to 1. The following correspondences will be used:

push(1)	$k{:=}k*2$
push(2)	$k{:=}k*2+1$
topofstack=2	$odd(k)$
emptystack	$k=1$
pop	$k{:=}k$ **div** 2

The procedure thus becomes:

```
procedure p ;
begin integer k ;
      k:=1 ;
BEG : while cond do begin A ; k:=k*2 end ;
      D ;
      while k≠1 and odd(k) do
      begin k:=k div 2 ; C end ;
      if k≠1 then
      begin B ; k:=k+1 ; goto BEG end
end
```

6.3.2.3. *Exercises*

(1) Write procedures *triangles*2 and *band* (5.5.2) in an iterative form.

(2) (a) Calculate the amount of storage space needed for executing the recursive procedure of sorting by partitioning (5.4.1) in the best and worst case. Compare with the recursive procedure of section 6.2.3.1 and the iterative procedure of section 6.3.2.1.

(b) Write a recursive procedure for sorting by partitioning such that the storage space required is, in the worst case, of the order of the logarithm of the number of elements in the array.

(*Hint*: The order in which the recursive calls of procedure 5.4.1 are executed is arbitrary. This procedure can be rewritten in such a way that, after elimination of tail recursion, the remaining recursive call deals with the smallest sub-array.)

(c) Write the procedure obtained in (b) in an iterative form. Analyse the storage space required for its execution and compare it with previous procedures.

6.4. Examples

6.4.1. The towers of Hanoi

The towers of Hanoi is a game invented in the nineteenth century by Edward Lucas. It is played with three rods, A, B, and C, and a certain number of discs of different diameters, with holes in the middle which allow them to be put on the rods. This is how it starts:

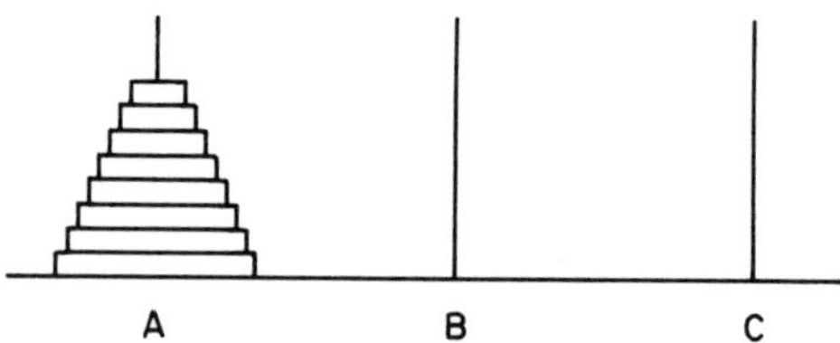

The discs are stacked in order of decreasing size on rod A, thus forming the figure called 'tower of Hanoi', hence the name of the game. The aim is to transfer the tower on rod A to rod B, making use of rod C as an intermediary, in other words, to finish up as shown below.

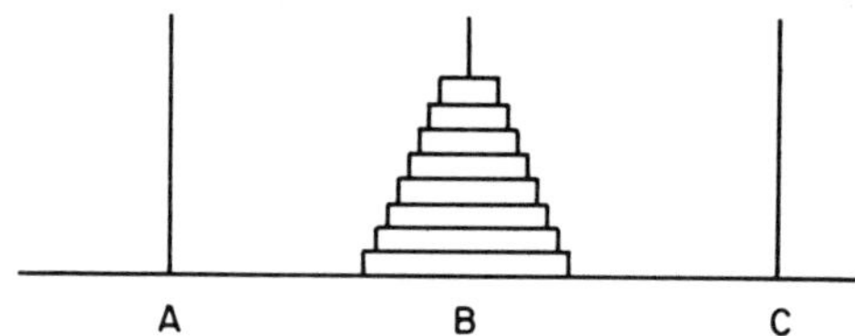

The one and only permissible move is to take a disc from the top of one tower and to put it on another rod to form another tower; putting a disc on the ground or on another, larger disc is not allowed.

Let $n > 0$ be the number of discs in the game, and *move*(a,b) the primitive for manipulating the discs, meaning 'take the disc at the top of the tower on rod a, and put it on rod b'.

6.4.1.1. *Recursive program*

If $n = 1$, the solution is obvious: we simply have to execute *move*(A, B).

If $n > 1$, we begin by transferring a tower of height $(n-1)$ from rod A to rod C, using B as an intermediary. Then, *move*(A, B) brings the largest disc to its final resting place. To finish, we still have to transfer the tower of height $(n-1)$ on rod C to rod B, using A as an intermediary.

This decomposition leads to the following recursive procedure:

```
procedure hanoi (rod value a, b, c ; integer value n) ;
if n = 1 then move (a,b)
else begin
     hanoi (a, c, b, n−1) ;
     move (a, b) ;
     hanoi (c, b, a, n−1)
     end
```

Exercise

Show that a call *hanoi*(. . . , n) invokes 2^n-1 executions of the primitive *move* . According to Lucas, there is a temple at Benares where the priests have spent their time since the Creation transferring a tower of 64 discs. Knowing that the world will end when their task is finished, calculate the lifespan of the universe.

6.4.1.2. *Iterative program*

By eliminating the parameters, we obtain the following program:

```
rod a,b,c, ; integer n ;
procedure hanoi ;
if n = 1 then move(a,b)
else begin
     b :=: c ; n:=n−1 ;
     hanoi ;
     b :=: c ; move(a,b) ; a :=: c ;
     hanoi ;
     a :=: c ; n:=n+1
     end
```

Remark 1. We have used inverse functions rather than a stack to restore parameter values after each of the recursive calls.

Procedure *hanoi*, when written in this way, restores the original values of a, b, c, and n.

Remark 2. Since the primitives *move* and :=: do not use the value of n, we have replaced the sequence:

$b :=: c$; $n:=n+1$; *move*(a,b) ; $a :=: c$; $n:=n-1$

by the equivalent sequence:

$b :=: c$; *move*(a,b) ; $a :=: c$

The procedure obtained by elimination of recursion follows a similar pattern to the example discussed in §6.3.2.2. It can take one of two forms, as follows:

```
rod a,b,c ; integer n ;
procedure hanoi ;
    begin
E : while n ≠ 1 do begin b :=: c ; n:=n−1 ; push(1) end ;
    move(a,b) ;
    while (¬ emptystack andiftrue topofstack = 2) do
      begin pop ; a :=: c ; n:=n+1 end
    if ¬ emptystack then
      begin pop ; b :=: c ; move(a,b) ;
              a :=: c ; push (2) ; goto E
      end
end
```

or:

```
rod a,b,c ; integer n ;
procedure hanoi ;
    begin integer k ; k:=1 ;
E : while n ≠ 1 do begin b :=: c ; n:=n−1 ; k:=k*2 end ;
    move(a,b) ;
    while k≠1 and odd(k) do
    begin k:=k div 2 ; a :=: c ; n:=n+1 end
   if k≠1 then
    begin b :=: c ; move(a,b) ; a :=: c ;
            k:=k+1 ; goto E
    end
   end
```

When the stack is represented by an integer variable, whose maximum value is *maxint*, the size of the stack is bounded by $\log_2(maxint)$.

For instance, if the integers are coded in a binary representation on 32 bits, the stack will have a maximum size of 32. The corresponding procedure *hanoi* can then be executed only if $n \leqslant 32$. This limitation is not unreasonable since the number of moves is an exponential function of n (see exercise 6.4.1.1).

Exercise

Suppose $n_0 > 0$ is the initial value of variable n. Show that, in the preceding program, the relation $2^{n_0-n} \leqslant k < 2^{n_0-n+1}$ is true for each evaluation of the test $n \neq 1$. Derive from this a version of procedure *hanoi* in which the value of n is not modified.

6.4.1.3. *Optimizations*

We are going to transform the above program so as to reduce the number of :=: operations.

Consider the loop:

while $n \neq 1$ **do begin** b :=: c ; n :=n−1 ; k := k∗2 **end**

This loop is executed $n - 1$ times. The values b and c are therefore exchanged $n - 1$ times: if n is even, this is equivalent to a single exchange; if n is odd, the values stay the same. We can therefore replace the loop by the following sequence:

if *even*(n) **then** b :=: c ; k :=k∗(2 ↑ (n−1)) ; n:=1

Consider also the loop:

while $k \neq 1$ **and** *odd*(k) **do**
begin k:=k **div** 2 ; a :=: c ; n:=n+1 **end**

The value of n before execution of the loop is always 1. The loop can be replaced by the sequence:

while $k \neq 1$ **and** *odd*(k) **do begin** k:=k **div** 2 ; n:=n+1 **end**
if *even*(n) **then** a :=: c

From this we can derive the following program:

```
rod a,b,c ; integer n ;
procedure hanoi ;
   begin integer k ; k:=1 ;
E : if even(n) then b :=: c ;
    move(a,b) ;
    k := k*(2 ↑ (n−1)) ;
    n := 1 ;
    while k≠ 1 and odd(k) do
    begin k:=k div 2 ; n:=n+1 end ;
    if k≠ 1 then
    begin
       if even(n) then a :=: c ;
       b :=: c ;
       move(a,b) ;
       a :=: c ;
       k := k+1 ; goto E
    end
   end
```

Exercise 1

In the above procedure, two or four :=: instructions are executed at each iteration, depending on the evenness of n. Transform the procedure so that these operations are replaced by exactly four assignments at each iteration.

Exercise 2

Suppose we introduce an integer variable i into procedure *hanoi*. This variable is initialized to 1 at the same time as k. It is increased by 1 before the jump to label E: we then have the sequence $k{:=}k+1$; $i{:=}i+1$; **goto** E.

(a) Let n_0 be the initial value of variable n. Show that the equation $k-i = 2^{n_0-1} - 1$ is always true after execution of the assignment $k := k*(2\uparrow(n-1))$.

(b) Show that the loop
while $k \neq 1$ **and** $odd(k)$ **do begin** $k{:=}k$ **div** 2 ; $n{:=}n+1$ **end**
can then be replaced by the sequence
$j{:=}i$;
while $even(j)$ **do begin** $j{:=}j$ **div** 2 ; $n{:=}n+1$ **end**.

(c) Modify the procedure obtained so as to eliminate variable k, without changing the value of n.

By bringing together the results of these two exercises, we end up with the following procedure:

```
rod a, b, c ; integer n ;
procedure hanoi ;
   begin integer i, j, m ; Boolean p ; rod x ;
     i:=1 ; p:=even(n) ; m:=2 ↑ (n−1) ;
     if p then b :=: c ;
E :  move(a,b) ; j:=i ; p:=false ;
     while even(j) do begin j:=j div 2 ; p:=¬p end ;
     if i ≠ m then
     begin x:=a ; a:=b ; b:=c ; c:=x ;
       if p then move(b,c) else move(c,b) ;
       i:=i+1 ; goto E
     end
end
```

6.4.2. The Schorr and Waite algorithm

6.4.2.1. *Marking algorithms*

We are given:

- a set of records with the following structure:
  record *vertex* (**Boolean** *mark* ; **pointer**(*vertex*) $f1, f2$)
- a (*vertex*) **pointer** *source*, *which designates one of the records.*

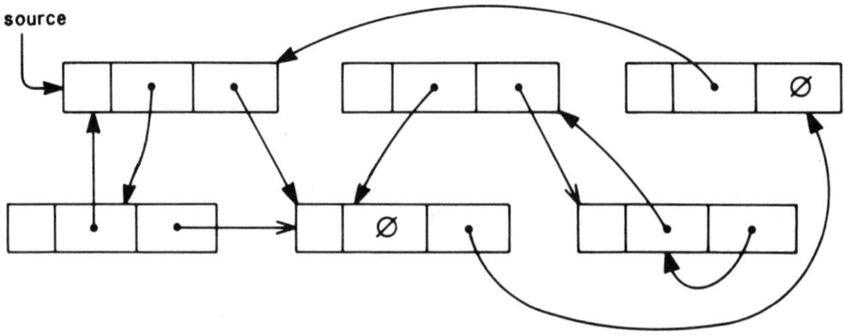

Example

Suppose the *mark* field of each record initially has the value *falsee*. The problem consists in assigning the value *true* to the *mark* field of each record which can be reached from the source, that is to say, records designated by *source*, *f*1(*source*), *f*2(*source*), *f*1(*f*1(*source*)), *f*1(*f*2(*source*)), ... etc. An algorithm for solving this problem is called a marking algorithm.

A classic application of marking algorithms is the management of storage space for records: when there is no more free space available, one executes a program called *garbage-collection*, which marks all the records reachable from existing variables; the records which remain unmarked are no longer usable, and the space they occupy can be made available for reuse.

6.4.2.2. *Writing a recursive marking procedure*

The problem of marking is similar to that of traversing a graph (§5.6.1), where the set of records is taken to represent a graph. The graph in question may, however, be cyclic.

Let us write a procedure similar to procedure *maxweight*2 in §5.6.1.2:

```
procedure mark1 (pointer(vertex) value x) ;
if x ≠ nil andiftrue ¬ mark(x) then
begin
   mark1(f1(x)) ;
   mark1(f2(x)) ;
   mark(x) := true
end
```

According to the results of Chapter 5, this procedure is correct whenever the graph is acyclic. However, if the graph contains a cycle, then it is clear that the procedure may not terminate. To ensure termination, we simply have to avoid traversing any cycle more than once, for instance by marking vertices as soon as they are encountered.

The set $R(S,x)$ of vertices reachable from x without passing through a vertex of S is such that:

$$R(S,x) = \emptyset \qquad \text{if } x = nil \text{ or } x \in S$$
$$= \{x\} \cup R(S \cup \{x\}, f1(x)) \cup R(S \cup \{x\} \cup R(S \cup \{x\}, f1(x)), f2(x))$$
otherwise

(*Exercise*: Check that this definition is equivalent to that given in section 5.6.1.2.)

Using the property proved in section 5.6.1.2, we can modify the above equation to express $R(S,x)$ as the union of disjoint sets:

$$R(S,x) = \emptyset \qquad \text{if } x = nil \text{ or } x \in S$$
$$= \{x\} \cup R(S \cup \{x\}, f1(x))$$
$$\cup R(S \cup \{x\} \cup R(S \cup \{x\}, f1(x)), f2(x)) \text{ otherwise}$$

From this we derive the following procedure:

```
procedure mark2 (pointer(vertex) value x) ;
if x ≠ nil andiftrue ¬ mark(x) then
begin
   mark(x) := true ;
   mark2(f1(x)) ;
   mark2(f2(x))
end
```

According to the preceding decomposition, this procedure is partially correct. The number of records which are unmarked and reachable from the source is strictly decreasing along every path of the call tree. The procedure therefore terminates and is totally correct.

6.4.2.3. *Analysis of procedure mark2*

Let n be the number of records which can be reached from the source.

Calculation of execution time

The instruction *mark*(x) := *true* is executed n times exactly.

So there are $2n$ recursive calls.

The condition $x \neq nil$ **andiftrue** $\neg$ *mark*(x) is evaluated $2n+1$ times (once for the principal call and once for each recursive call). Note that it returns *true* n times and *false* $n+1$ times.

The execution time of mark2 is therefore of the order of the number of vertices which can be reached.

Analysis of storage requirements

Let N be the amount of storage space required (in addition to the records themselves) for executing *mark*2(source).

The value of N is proportional to the maximum number of embedded calls of *mark*2 for the principal call *mark*2(source).

The worst case is obtained when, for each call *mark*2(u), the set of vertices marked by one of two recursive calls *mark*2(*f*1(u)) and *mark*2(*f*2(u)) is empty. This is the case, for example, when the records form a linear list. The number of embedded calls is then $n+1$. The best case is obtained when, for each call *mark*2(u), the sets of vertices marked by *mark*2(*f*1(u)) and *mark*2(*f* 2(u)) contain the same number of elements. This is the case, for example, when the records form a complete binary tree. The number of embedded calls is then $\lceil \log_2 (n+1) \rceil + 1$.

For each call of *mark*2, we stack the value of parameter x and a return address. If a store location can contain an address, we obtain:

$$2(\lceil \log_2 (n+1) \rceil + 1) \leqslant N \leqslant 2(n+1)$$

We must therefore have $2n+2$ store locations to be able to guarantee the execution of *mark2(source)*.

This requirement is a hindrance if the marking procedure is used by a garbage-collection program, which is called by definition when there is no more space available. By transforming *mark2* into an iterative procedure, we shall now produce a solution which uses up less space.

6.4.2.4. *Transforming mark2 into a procedure without parameters*

```
pointer(vertex) x ;
procedure mark3 ;
if x ≠ nil andiftrue ¬ mark(x) then
begin
   mark(x) := true ;
   push(x) ; x := f1(x) ; mark3 ; pop(x) ;
   push(x) ; x := f2(x) ; mark3 ; pop(x)
end
```

This procedure obviously requires as much storage space as *mark2*, since all we have done is to make explicit the implicit stack of parameter values.

To reduce the amount of space needed, we can eliminate this stack, which in fact just contains the sequence of vertices on the path traversed from the source to the current vertex. This can be done by a 'pointer reversal' technique, already used for a linear list by the program *PL2* of section 2.3.2.

In what follows, x designates the current vertex, and y its predecessor on the path traversed from the point of origin. On execution of the instruction *mark*(x) := *true*, we have:

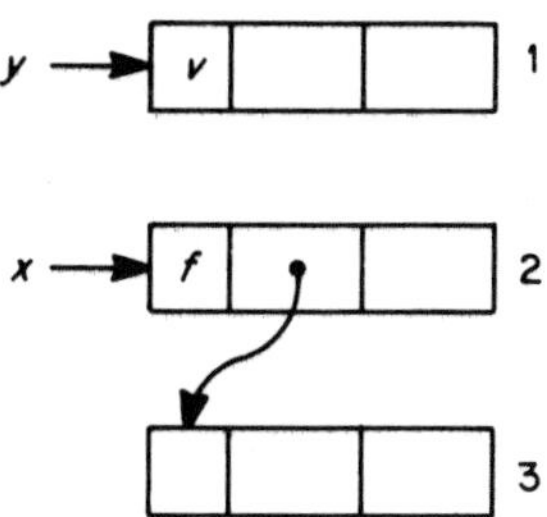

Figure 1 (in which the field $f1$ or $f2$ of record 1 which points to x has been inverted)

Before executing the first recursive call, we must have:

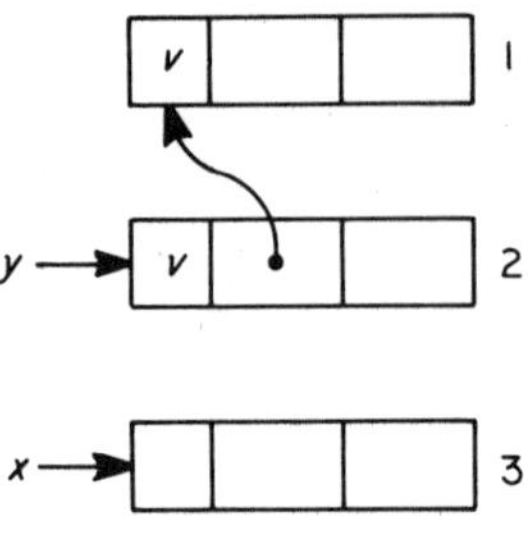

Figure 2

It is therefore sufficient to replace the sequence *push*(x) ; x:=$f1(x)$ by

(*) $z := y \; ; y := x \; ; x := f1(y) \; ; f1(y) := z$

where z is an auxiliary variable of type **pointer**(*vertex*).

Let us assume: (h) The recursive calls of procedure *mark*3 restore the values of x, y and fields $f1$ and $f2$ for all records.

The instruction *pop*(x) may then be replaced by

(**) $z := x \; ; x := y \; ; y := f1(x) \; ; f1(x) := z$.

Let us denote the sequence (*) by $A_{x,y,f1}$. The sequence (**) can then be written $A_{y,x,f1}$. The sequence

$A_{x,y,f1}$; *mark*3 ; $A_{y,x,f1}$

restores the connections of Figure 1, provided (h) is true. The sequences to be executed before and after the second recursive call *mark*3 are $A_{x,y,f2}$ and $A_{y,x,f2}$ respectively.

We then have the property:

if (h) is true, then the execution of the body of procedure *mark*3 restores the initial values of the pointers.

From this it can be inferred that every call of *mark*3 restores the values of the pointers.

Consequently:

(h) is true;

the principal call of *mark*3 restores the connections of the original graph.

The following program is obtained:

```
pointer(vertex) x,y,z ;
procedure mark4 ;
if x ≠ nil andiftrue ¬ mark(x) then
begin
   mark(x) := true ;
   A_{x,y,f1} ; mark4 ; A_{y,x,f1} ;
   A_{x,y,f2} ; mark4 ; A_{y,x,f2}
end
```

The principal call is written: $x := source$; $y := nil$; *mark*4.

Remarks

The stack of *mark*3 is replaced by the sequence of fields whose pointers are reversed; *y* denotes the head of the stack.
The sequence $A_{y,x,f1}$; $A_{x,y,f2}$ can be reduced to
$z := f1(y)$; $f1(y) := x$; $x := f2(y)$; $f2(y) := z$.

Exercise

(1) Eliminate tail recursion from procedure *mark*1.
(2) Calculate the amount of storage space needed to execute the program.
(3) Transform the derived procedure into a recursive procedure without parameters. Show that the method of 'pointer reversal' cannot be used to replace the stack.

6.4.2.5. *Eliminating recursion*

Procedure *mark*4 uses a stack of return addresses, whereas *mark*2 uses a stack of return addresses and pointers. There are only three return addresses: a stack of bits is therefore adequate, since the end of the principal call can be determined by the test for an empty stack. A stack of bits is needed, since the values of the pointers at the end of the procedure do not allow us to distinguish between the two recursive calls. On the other hand, representing the stack by an integer variable will not be a practical proposition, as this would severely limit the depth of the recursion.

Procedure *mark*4 takes the same form as procedure *hanoi*, and is written iteratively:

```
pointer(vertex) x,y,z ;
procedure mark5 ;
begin
E :   while x ≠ nil andiftrue ¬ mark(x) do
      begin mark(x) := true ; z := y ; y := x ;
            x := f1(y) ; f1(y) := z ; push(false)
      end ;
      while ¬ emptystack andiftrue topofstack = true do
      begin pop ; z := x ; x := y ;
            y := f2(x) ; f2(x) := z
      end ;
      if ¬ emptystack then
      begin pop ; z := f1(y) ; f1(y) := x ; x := f2(y) ;
            f2(y) := z ; push(true) ; goto E
      end
end
```

Remark

The test ¬ *emptystack* can be replaced by $y \neq nil$ (see the remark in § 6.4.2.4).

In garbage collection programs which make use of this algorithm, the stack of bits is often replaced by a mark added on to each record. Usually, this takes up more space than the stack although, in the worst case, the space used is the same. We now give a marking program for records with the following structure:

record(*vertex*) (**Boolean** *mark*, *call*2 ; **pointer**(*vertex*) *f*1,*f*2)

where the Boolean *call*2 replaces the stack.

```
pointer(vertex) x,y,z ;
procedure mark6 ;
begin
E :   while x ≠ nil andiftrue ¬ mark(x) do
      begin mark(x) := true ; z := y ; y := x ;
            x:=f1(y) ; f1(y) := z ; call2(y) := false
      end ;
      while y ≠ nil andiftrue call2(y) do
      begin z := x ; x := y ;
            y := f2(x) ; f2(x) := z
      end ;
      if y ≠ nil then
      begin z := f1(y) ; f1(y) := x ; x := f2(y) ;
            f2(y) := z ; call2(y) := true ; goto E
      end
end
```

The principal call is written:

$x := source$; $y := nil$; *mark*6

The test *emptystack* is replaced by $y = nil$.

(Note that $x = source$ would be incorrect.)

Exercises

(1) We can reduce the number of procedure calls by modifying procedure *mark*2 so as to eliminate the calls for which either x has the value *nil*, or x is marked. Write this procedure, and transform it into an iterative program.

(2) Write a marking program using a stack of bounded depth and pointer reversal when the stack is full.

(3) Generalize the Schorr and Waite algorithm for marking sets of records which contain an arbitrary number of fields of type pointer (the Deutsch algorithm).

6.5. Elimination of recursion and the ordering of computations

The transformations presented so far do not modify the computations performed by recursive programs. They do not allow us to eliminate computations invoked by recursive calls which may in fact be redundant.

For example, the transformation of procedure *combination*1 (§ 5.6.2) leads to an iterative program which is just as inefficient; and we have seen how, by performing a traversal and marking the call-graph, to get to a recursive program with no redundant computations. The derived recursive program, *combination*2, carries out a topological sort of the vertices in the graph. The order of vertices is the same as that given by procedure *topsort* of section 5.6.3.

Every topological order is, however, compatible with the partial ordering imposed by the graph for the calculation of recursive calls. Now, the order C_1^0 C_1^1 C_2^0 C_2^1 C_2^2 C_3^0, etc. is a topological order. It is easy to write an iterative program which enumerates the vertices of the call-graph according to this order and which calculates C_n^p, using an array of integers called *c*:

```
for i := 1 to n do
for j := max(0,p+i−n) to min(i,p) do
    c(i,j) := if j = 0 or j = i then 1
              else c(i−1,j) + c(i−1,j−1)
```

In this way, we produce a program which is simpler than that obtained by transforming procedure *combination*2 according to the methods described earlier. The term 'dynamic programming' is often associated with this method of eliminating recursion.

In many examples of recursive procedures, it is possible to write simple iterative programs for the topological sorting of the graph of calls. Even if there are no redundant computations, it can be interesting to eliminate recursion by 'dynamic programming'.

Exercise

Consider an array $T(1::N)$ of integers, to be sorted in order of increasing size. We use the following recursive decomposition:

To sort $T(inf::sup)$, with $inf < sup$, we sort

$$T\left(inf::\frac{inf+sup}{2}\right) \quad \text{and} \quad T\left(\frac{inf+sup}{2}+1::sup\right),$$

and then we merge the two sorted sub-arrays.

(1) Write

a procedure *sort*(*inf*,*sup*) which makes use of this decomposition;

a procedure *merge*(*inf*,*i*,*sup*) which merges the two sub-arrays $T(inf::i)$

and $T(i+1::sup)$, in a time of order $n = sup - inf + 1$. (Extra storage space of size order n can be used.)

(2) Transform procedure *sort* into an iterative program:
using the general method presented in section 6.3;
using the method presented in this section.

(3) Calculate the execution time of the different procedures.

Comments and Bibliography

The importance of transforming recursive programs into iterative programs, as a method of programming, has been demonstrated by Knuth (1974).

The transformations studied in this chapter allow us to eliminate inefficiencies produced by compilers for recursive languages. In the example of the towers of Hanoi, we were eventually able to produce a simpler program by transforming to an iterative program. This example is discussed in more detail by Arsac (1983). The Schorr and Waite algorithm is studied by Knuth (1969). In this example, it is the amount of storage space used which is optimized by program transformation.

The transformations outlined in section 6.5 permit more ambitious optimizations. They are similar to the transformations of recursive programs discussed in Chapter 5 (see Burstall and Darlington, 1977; Bird, 1980).

Appendix 1

Notes on the Language used for Writing Programs

This language is close to PASCAL, but we have borrowed the following ideas from ALGOLW:

the concept of block (see section 3.3.2)

the syntax of declarations

the syntax of expressions which use pointers and records (see section 2.3).

Procedure declarations are described in section 3.4.1.

We also use the following symbols:

¬	¬ *a*, where *a* is of type **Boolean**, has value *not*(*a*).
div	*a* **div** *b*, where *a* and *b* are of type **integer**, has value $\lfloor a/b \rfloor$.
↑	*a* ↑ *b*, where *a* and *b* are of type **integer**, has value a^b.
andiftrue	*a* **andiftrue** *b*, where *a* and *b* are of type **Boolean**, is equivalent to: **if** *a* **then** *b* **else** *false* . (Evaluation of *a* **andiftrue** *b* gives the same result as that of *a* **and** *b*, except when evaluation of *a* gives *false*, and *b* is undefined.)
oriffalse	*a* **oriffalse** *b*, where *a* and *b* are of type **Boolean**, is equivalent to: **if** ¬ *a* **then** *b* **else** *true* . (Evaluation of *a* **oriffalse** *b* gives the same result as that of *a* **or** *b*, except when evaluation of *a* gives *true*, and *b* is undefined.)
:=:	*a* :=: *b*, where *a* and *b* are two variables of the same type, exchanges the values of *a* and *b*.
even	*even*(*a*), where *a* is of type **integer**, has the value *true* if the value of *a* is even, *false* if it is odd.
odd	*odd*(*a*), where *a* is of type **integer**, has the value *true* if the value of *a* is odd, *false* if it is even.

Finally, we use the following primitives: *push*, *pop*, *emptystack* (sections 2.3.1 and 3.3.4), *swap* (section 2.2), *topofstack* (section 6.3.2.2), *place*, *trace* (section 5.2), *move* (section 6.4.1).

Appendix 2

Definitions of the Graph-theoretic Terms used in Chapters 5 and 6

The term *graph* denotes a pair $\langle X,\Gamma\rangle$, where X is any set, and Γ is a subset of $X \times X$.

X is called the set of *vertices*, and Γ the set of *edges* in the graph.

Given an edge(x, y), x is the *source* and y the *target* of the edge. For every vertex x, we denote by $\Gamma(x)$ the set of target vertices of edges with source x.

The graph $\langle X,\Gamma\rangle$ is said to be *finite* or *infinite* according to whether the set X of vertices is finite or infinite.

In a graph, a *path* is a sequence of vertices $x_0, x_1, \ldots, x_k$, with $k \geqslant 0$, such that for all i, $0 \leqslant i \leqslant k-1$, there exists an edge with source x_i and target x_{i+1}.

x_0 is called the *origin* of the path, and x_k the *destination* of the path. Integer k is the *length* of the path.

For each vertex x of a graph, there exists a path of zero length with origin x.

Remark

A path of length $k \geqslant 1$ may also be defined as a sequence of edges $u_1, u_2, \ldots, u_k$ such that, for all i, $1 \leqslant i \leqslant k-1$, the source of u_{i+1} is equal to the target of u_i.

The term *cycle* denotes a path of non-zero length whose origin and destination are identical.

A vertex z is *reachable* from a vertex x if and only if there exists a path with origin x and destination z.

Bibliography

Aho, A. V., J. E. Hopcroft, and J. D. Ullman (1974) *The Design and Analysis of Computer Algorithms*, Addison-Wesley.

Aho, A. V., J. E. Hopcroft, and J. D. Ullman (1983) *Data Structures and Algorithms*, Addison-Wesley.

Alagic, S., and M. A. Arbib (1978) *The Design of Well-structured and Correct Programs*, Springer-Verlag.

Apt, K. R. (1981) Ten years of Hoare's logic: a survey—Part 1, *ACM Trans. on Programming Languages and Systems*, **3**, 431–483.

Arbib, M. A., A. J. Kfoury, and R. N. Moll (1981) *A Basis for Theoretical Computer Science*, Springer-Verlag.

Arsac, J. (1980) *Premières Leçons de programmation,* CEDIC/Fernand Nathan.

Arsac, J. (1983) *Les Bases de la programmation*, Dunod.

Banachowski, L., A. Kreczmar, G. Mirkowska, H. Rasiowa, and A. Salwicki (1977) An introduction to algorithmic logic; metamathematical investigations in the theory of programs. In *Mathematical Foundations of Computer Science* (Mazurkiewitcz and Pawlak, ed.), Banach Center Publications, Warsaw.

Biondi, J., and G. Clavel (1981) *Introduction à la programmation,* Masson.

Bird, R. S. (1980) Tabulation techniques for recursive programs, *ACM Computing Surveys*, **12**(4), 403–417.

Burstall, R. M. (1969) Proving properties of programs by structural induction, *Computing Journal*, **12**(1), 41–48.

Burstall, R. M. (1974) Program proving as hand simulation with a little induction. In *Information Processing*, North-Holland, pp. 308–312.

Burstall, R. M., and J. Darlington (1977) A transformation system for developing recursive programs, *J. ACM,* **24**(1), 44–61.

Courtin, J., and J. Voiron (1974) Introduction à l'algorithmique et aux structures de données. Cyclostyled lecture notes, IUT B, Grenoble.

Dijkstra, E. W. (1976) *A Discipline of Programming,* Prentice-Hall.

Floyd, R. W. (1967) Assigning meaning to programs, *Proc. AMS Symposium in Applied Mathematics*, **19**, pp. 19–31.

Gerbier, A. (1977) Mes premières constructions de programmes, *Lecture Notes in Computer Science*, 55, Springer-Verlag.

Greene, D. H., and D. E. Knuth (1981) *Mathematics for the Analysis of Algorithms*, Birkhauser.

Gries, D. (1981) *The Science of Programming*, Springer-Verlag.

Harel, D. (1979) First-order dynamic logic, *Lecture Notes in Computer Science*, 68, Springer-Verlag.

Harel, D. (1980) Proving the correctness of regular deterministic programs: a unifying survey using dynamic logic, *Theoretical Computer Science,* **12**, 61–81.

Hoare, C. A. R. (1969) An axiomatic basis for computer programming, *Comm. ACM,* **12**(10), 576–580 and 583.

Hoare, C. A. R. (1971) Procedures and parameters: an axiomatic approach, *Lecture Notes in Mathematics*, 188, Springer-Verlag, pp. 102–116.
Kleene, S. C. (1967) *Mathematical Logic*, Wiley.
Knuth, D. E. (1969) *The Art of Computer Programming, Vol. 1: Fundamental Algorithms,* Addison-Wesley.
Knuth, D. E. (1973) *The Art of Computer Programming, Vol. 3: Sorting and Searching,* Addison-Wesley.
Knuth, D. E. (1974) Structured programming with Go To statements, *ACM Computing Surveys*, **6**(4), 261–301.
Laurent, J. P. (1982) *Initiation à l'analyse et à la programmation,* Dunod.
Liu, C. L. (1977) *Elements of Discrete Mathematics*, McGraw-Hill.
Livercy, C. (1978) *Théorie des programmes,* Dunod.
Lucas, M., J. P. Peyrin, and P. C. Scholl (1983) *Algorithmique et représentation des données, Vol 1: Files et automates,* Masson.
Mahl, R., and J. C. Boussard (1983) *Algorithmique et structure de données,* Eyrolles.
Manna, Z. (1974) *Mathematical Theory of Computation*, McGraw-Hill.
Manna, Z., and R. Waldinger (1978) Is "sometime" better than "always"? Intermittent assertions in proving program correctness, *Comm. ACM,* **21**(2).
Meyer, B., and C. Baudoin (1978) *Méthodes de programmation*, Eyrolles.
Pair, C. (1978) La programmation; de l'énoncé au programme. AFCET Computer Science Congress, Gif-sur-Yvette.
Sedgewick, R. (1977) The analysis of quicksort programs, *Acta Informatica,* **7**, 327–355.
Stanat, D. F., and D. F. McAllister (1977) *Discrete Mathematics in Computer Science*, Prentice-Hall.
Tarjan, T. E. (1978) Complexity of combinatorial algorithms, *SIAM Review*, **20**(3), 457–491.
Veillon, G. (1974) Algorithmique. Cyclostyled lecture notes, IMAG.
Wirth, N. (1976) *Algorithms + Data Structures = Programs,* Prentice-Hall.
Wirth, N. (1972) *Systematic Programming: An Introduction.* Prentice-Hall.

List of Programs Presented in the Text

Demco, Inc. 38-293

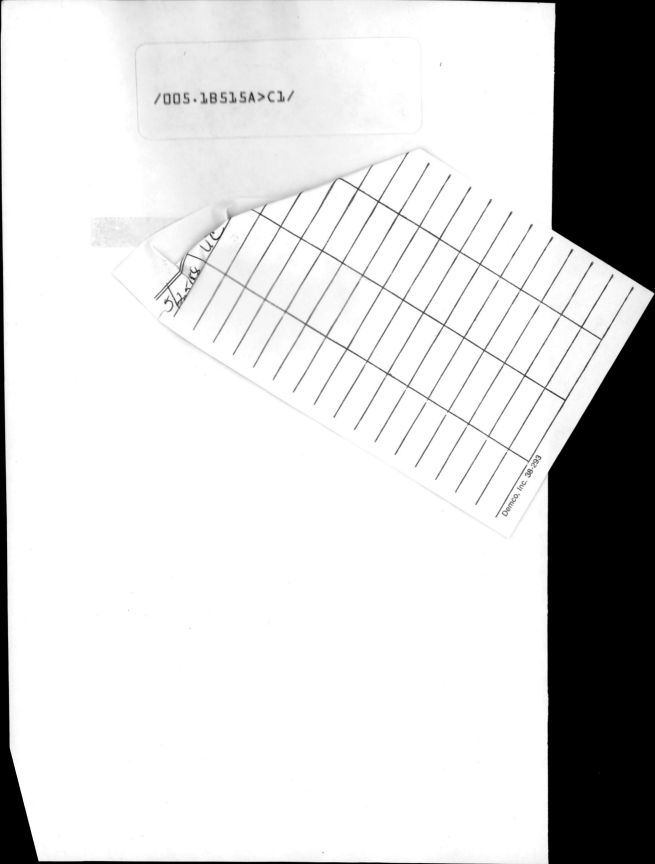